SIERRA LEONE

INTERNATIONAL PEACE ACADEMY
OCCASIONAL PAPER SERIES

SIERRA LEONE

Diamonds and the Struggle for Democracy

John L. Hirsch

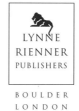

LYNNE
RIENNER
PUBLISHERS

BOULDER
LONDON

Published in the United States of America in 2001 by
Lynne Rienner Publishers, Inc.
1800 30th Street, Boulder, Colorado 80301
www.rienner.com

and in the United Kingdom by
Lynne Rienner Publishers, Inc.
3 Henrietta Street, Covent Garden, London WC2E 8LU

Library of Congress Cataloging-in-Publication Data
Hirsch, John L., 1936–
    Sierra Leone : diamonds and the struggle for democracy / by John L. Hirsch.
        p. cm.—(International Peace Academy occasional paper series)
    Includes bibliographical references (p.) and index.
    ISBN 1-55587-698-6 (alk. paper)
      I. Title. II. Series.
    DT516.826.H57   2000
    966.4—dc21

                                            00-062563

British Cataloguing in Publication Data
A Cataloguing in Publication record for this book
is available from the British Library.

Contents

Illustrations

MAPS

PHOTOGRAPHS

Foreword

David Malone

The publication of this volume affords great pride to the International Peace Academy. IPA Occasional Papers have, over the years, examined a number of challenges to international peace and the ways in which they have been or could have been addressed. In most cases, the authors were primarily distinguished scholars and analysts.

John Hirsch, IPA vice-president, brings to this examination of the current crisis in Sierra Leone not only superb academic credentials but also the unrivaled vantage point of his tenure as Ambassador of the United States of America in Freetown from 1995 to 1998, during which a number of the events chronicled in the ensuing pages unfolded. His previous assignments in Africa prepared him well for the challenges he faced in Sierra Leone. Nothing prepared him so well as his love for the continent, which, in due course, also fostered great affection for Sierra Leone and its inhabitants.

Those who read this volume in draft all encouraged Hirsch to provide it with a more personal flavor than is mostly the case with scholarly work. His deeply held convictions and thoughtful conclusions on this continuing crisis, it seemed to us, would be of significant interest to all those who are committed to the resolution of Africa's ongoing conflicts. That he obliged us is a source of great satisfaction.

In this volume, Hirsch surveys the recent history of Sierra Leone and successive diplomatic initiatives that have failed to bring lasting peace to the country. He casts the crisis as regional rather than merely internal to Sierra Leone. He concludes with a number of policy and practical recommendations for a more convincing approach by regional and international actors, aimed at providing a stable framework for peacebuilding in Sierra Leone. The volume draws not only on recent developments on the ground but also on the latest policy developments at the UN and elsewhere. This volume will be of great value to practitioners and scholars alike, in Africa, key capitals, centers of learning, and at the United Nations.

Acknowledgments

At various stages of writing this account I have benefited greatly from the critical judgment and advice of a number of people. At the International Peace Academy, President David Malone has given me unstinting support and encouragement; Elizabeth Cousens and Adekeye Adebajo provided valuable analytical commentary as the text evolved; Florence Musaffi and Ciara Knudsen provided essential research and administrative support. Among those most familiar with Sierra Leone, I am particularly grateful to Syl Cheney Coker and Joseph Opala, who generously shared their knowledge of the country's complex history, deepened my understanding of events and personalities, and assisted with the preparation of the chronology. Former United Nations special envoys Berhanu Dinka and Francis Okelo as well as Margaret Vogt and Kathryn Jones of the department of political affairs provided useful insights into the role of the United Nations throughout the decade.

Among my colleagues in the State Department, Howard Jeter, former U.S. special envoy for Liberia, and my successor, Ambassador Joseph Melrose, helped me to understand events before and after my term, and corrected the record on a number of important issues. I am also very grateful to Ed Brynn, Walter Carrington, Bill Milam, Tibor Nagy, Brenda Schoonover, and Lannon Walker, respectively U.S. ambassadors in Ghana, Nigeria, Liberia, Guinea, Togo, and Côte d'Ivoire, for their insights as well as their hospitality during my travels through the region. Ann Wright, who was in charge of the U.S. Embassy when the May 1997 coup took place, helped me to reconstruct those crucial days. Andrew Hillman at the U.S. Mission to the United Nations and Michael Thomas, Sierra Leone desk officer in the State Department, also provided invaluable assistance. Former Peace Corps volunteer Gary Schulze contributed the photographs from the 1996 election. Ann Grant at the Foreign Office in London and former High Commissioners Ian McCluney and Peter Penfold shared their perspectives on the British role in Sierra Leone during these years of crisis.

I am profoundly grateful for the friendship and hospitality of more Sierra Leoneans than I could possibly mention here. I would like to pay tribute to my U.S. and Sierra Leonean colleagues at the U.S. Embassy in Freetown for their unflagging commitment to the goal of a democratic and peaceful Sierra Leone. President Ahmed Tejan Kabbah's warm friendship throughout this time of national and personal travail remains an enduring memory. Leading members of civil society and innumerable others generously shared their insights and perspectives with me. Amy Smythe, Isha Dyfan, and Sheka Mansaray, who lived through these events, read the manuscript and offered valuable suggestions. Finally, I want to thank my wife, Rita, whose love and support have sustained me throughout my diplomatic career. I alone am responsible for the final text.

—*J. L. H.*

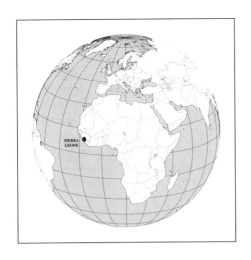

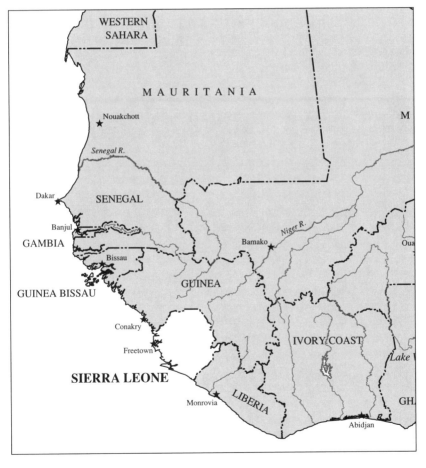

Sierra Leone

Introduction

This is an inquiry into the causes and consequences of Sierra Leone's traumatic conflict over the past decade. It is in part a story of flawed leadership and voracious greed, and of political failure at regional and international levels to prevent the tragedy that has befallen an entire population. It is also, however, the story of a democratic movement striving to rectify past practices, and of ongoing efforts by the United Nations and the Economic Community of West African States (ECOWAS) to restore peace to a devastated land. Sierra Leone presents Africa and the West with the most profound ethical and moral issues. The brutal violence that the Revolutionary United Front (RUF) inflicted on a defenseless population has sent a chilling reminder that the battle to defeat evil is never over.

In February 1995 the U.S. State Department offered me the opportunity to serve as ambassador to the Republic of Sierra Leone, a small country in West Africa scarcely known to most Americans. As I prepared for my assignment, I discovered that Sierra Leone had a direct connection with the United States as one of the principal departure points for the slave trade, particularly for the rice plantations of Georgia and South Carolina. The Gullah language and traditions still preserved on the coastal islands hark directly back to Sierra Leone. When British activity in the slave trade ended in 1808, Sierra Leone receded (from an American perspective) into obscurity as a remote British colony, even though it neighbored the only U.S. colonial enterprise in Africa, Liberia. In the nineteenth and early twentieth centuries, Sierra Leone acquired a positive reputation in West Africa based on its outstanding university and the high quality of its British-trained Krio civil servants. At independence, it was regarded as the "Athens of West Africa."

By 2000, however, Sierra Leone had joined Somalia, Rwanda, the Democratic Republic of Congo (DRC), Sudan, and Angola in the catalogue of states and societies ravaged by protracted conflict. The struggle between the RUF and three successive governments raged throughout the 1990s against the backdrop of three decades of state disintegration. But the relentless terror, loss of life, and indiscriminate amputations finally garnered international attention only after the coup of May 1997. Sierra Leone's collapse has deep and multiple roots. In this inquiry I seek to analyze the origins of the crisis, both historic and geographic, and then to explore a number of issues underlying the limited, delayed, and insufficient responses of the regional and international communities. The lessons to be drawn from the search for peace in Sierra Leone, highlighted in the following sections, are clearly relevant to the resolution of other ongoing crises in Africa and other areas of conflict.

Prevention of intrastate conflicts. Prevention has recently become a dominant concern of the United Nations, as well as a number of states and research institutions.[1] However, in the Sierra Leone case, over its forty-year history as an independent country there were no regional or international efforts to prevent the illegal exploitation of its natural resources or to address the collapse of its state institutions. There was no long-term structural intervention to address the profound gap between the few wealthy and powerful men at the top and the impoverished, malnourished, and uneducated majority. Diplomatic initiatives to prevent the war in Liberia from spilling over into Sierra Leone were negligible or nonexistent. The harsh reality is that Sierra Leone was a small, strategically insignificant country for its African neighbors and the broader international community. As we have repeatedly seen, inattention at early stages of political collapse almost always brings greater calamity later on.

Mediation of conflict. International attention has also focused on the importance of knowledgeable and sustained mediation as a key factor in resolving complex conflicts. From 1996 to 1999, three separate negotiations with the RUF failed to bring peace to Sierra Leone. The track records of those involved as mediators at different stages of the Sierra Leone crisis were mixed at best. The principal mediators were either chosen by interested states (the foreign ministers of Côte d'Ivoire and Nigeria) or assigned as available by overburdened regional and international institutions. These mediations took place in somewhat different contexts (in Abidjan and Lomé they aimed to end the rebel war; in Conakry to return the exiled president to power). The constant thread has been the inability of the regional and international communities to turn written undertakings into binding and enforceable agreements. The failure of these efforts (Lomé's outcome remains problematic) reflects above all the unwillingness, analytically and operationally, to relate the internal Sierra Leone crisis to the broader challenges of achieving regional peace. For both the United Nations and ECOWAS, Sierra Leone until May 1997 was the sideshow to the Liberian conflict. The RUF's ruthless authoritarian aspirations and the spoiler agenda of its external supporters—Liberia, Burkina Faso, and Libya—were perhaps understood but never effectively addressed. The limited political commitment of the "moral guarantors," the crosscutting agendas of Nigeria and Liberia, and the lack of adequate international resources have undermined effective implementation of all three agreements.

United Nations peace operations. The difficulties encountered by West African and United Nations peacekeepers in seeking to implement the Lomé Peace Agreement of July 1999 have again underscored the dangers inherent in Security Council decisions on deployment of peacekeeping forces without robust military capacity. Historically, the United Nations has been more successful in traditional peacekeeping than in complex peace enforcement. Despite early signs that the RUF would not voluntarily disarm and demobilize, a weak and poorly equipped United Nations force drawn from India and a number of African nations was deployed to Sierra Leone's hinterland. The evident gap between desired ends and available means quickly placed the peacekeepers in an untenable situation. There is clearly a need for the Security Council to reconsider its approach to Chapter VII enforcement operations. If UN peacemaking efforts are not to lose all credibility, the major powers need to be prepared to commit troops and financial resources rather than passing responsibility to African armies severely constrained by inadequate funding, training, and equipment.

Economic actors in civil conflicts. Underneath the political issues on the surface of the conflict are the economic factors that drove the war from the outset. Sierra Leone offers a prime example of an internal conflict where economic aspirations for control of valuable mineral resources, especially diamonds, have been largely responsible for its inception and protracted duration. The alluvial diamond fields of eastern Sierra Leone have been the main locus of fighting and the RUF's base of operations from the start. The connection between Liberian president Charles Taylor and RUF leader Foday Sankoh initially involved swaps of arms for diamonds. Both Taylor and Sankoh profited from continuation of the war, as did a number of arms dealers and diamond merchants who operated throughout the decade with impunity. The government's inability to regulate the diamond trade through official channels enabled Taylor and Sankoh to finance the war and reap huge gains by smuggling diamonds through Liberia and Côte d'Ivoire. The situation has not changed fundamentally since the signing of the Lomé Peace Agreement. Denying the RUF and Taylor access to the diamond resources is a fundamental requirement for ending the war.

Peace and justice. Ethnic cleansing in Bosnia and genocide in Rwanda have highlighted the complexity and importance of the quest for justice in postconflict situations and its relevance to the broader goal of reconciliation. The most controversial part of the Lomé agreement was the blanket amnesty. The RUF was freed from any legal responsibility under Sierra Leone's penal code for the deaths and atrocities that it inflicted on the civilian population from the start of the war in March 1991 to July 7, 1999.[2] UN Special Representative Francis Okelo appended a caveat to the agreement noting that, in the view of the United Nations, the amnesty does not apply to acts of genocide and crimes against humanity and has no validity in any case outside of Sierra Leone. Nonetheless the mediators, including the United Nations, believed that without the blanket amnesty the RUF would have withdrawn from the talks, leaving the bleak prospect of renewed fighting that none of the regional and international actors could stomach. As the RUF has continued to engage in acts of violence and commit atrocities since the Lomé agreement was signed, the international community has begun to address the need to deal with the perpetrators in a clear and unambiguous manner. The Security Council decision of August 14, 2000, to establish a war crimes tribunal to prosecute those responsible for the most grievous crimes against humanity and violations of international humanitarian law is an important step forward. Its implementation presents complex challenges for the Sierra Leone government and the international community as they seek to persuade the interim RUF leadership to end the decade-long war.

Private security forces. The prominent role of the South African security firm Executive Outcomes in the Sierra Leone crisis has highlighted the issue of private security forces' involvement in internal conflicts. The National Provisional Ruling Council (NPRC) needed Executive Outcomes in order to push the RUF forces back from within forty miles of the capital in May 1995. President Kabbah, following his election in March 1996, kept Executive Outcomes in the country until January 1997, two months after signing the Abidjan Accords. Less than four months later, rebel army units staged a coup and drove him into exile. A number of analysts concluded that Executive Outcomes was indispensable to stability in the absence of a loyal national army or any internationally mandated peace enforcement mission. Others have contended that such forces lack either ethics or accountability and as "hired guns" will only seek to exploit such conflicts for their own benefit.[3] Indeed, Executive Outcomes was linked with Branch Energy, a conglomerate of British, Canadian, and other business interests who had obtained kimberlite diamond concessions in eastern Sierra Leone. Yet the financial interests of Executive Outcomes aside, it is clear that President Kabbah made a fundamental mistake in requiring the security group to leave. The operational and moral issues raised by the use of private security forces in Sierra Leone are clearly relevant to crises elsewhere in Africa.

Postconflict recovery. Assisting Sierra Leone to recover from decades of corruption, mismanagement, and war poses a major challenge for the international community. In seeking to move from war to peace, Sierra Leone will remain dependent on outside support for both short-term recovery and medium-term development. International involvement on the security front is probably near its peak. The envisaged deployment of up to 20,500 United Nations peacekeepers from seven countries and 250 observers from thirty-two countries constitutes a significant level of engagement.[4] Yet prospects for financial resources to be provided for medium- to long-term recovery are poor. African leaders have correctly deplored the double standard of generous international support for Kosovo and East Timor compared to the meager amounts pledged to assist Sierra Leone and the DRC. The needs of other war-torn societies means there will inevitably be stiff competition for a limited pool of international assistance. Absent substantial support, Sierra Leone will remain a semipermanent ward of the international community. A modicum of stability and economic recovery is needed for even a small number of educated Sierra Leoneans residing abroad to return home. Regional and international partnerships with a weak government and a struggling civil society movement are thus being put to the test in the most fundamental way.

The grim events that have occurred in Sierra Leone were presaged in Robert Kaplan's widely read article in the February 1994 *Atlantic Monthly*, entitled "The Coming Anarchy." Kaplan presented Sierra Leone as the epicenter of anarchy in West Africa and a dire warning of the return to primitive societal conditions and uncontrolled warfare that awaited much of the third world. Kaplan's article appeared four months after eighteen U.S. Army rangers were killed in Mogadishu, triggering the U.S. withdrawal from Somalia, and two months before the start of the Rwanda crisis. His pessimistic prognosis buttressed the growing trend in the Washington policy community of withdrawal from direct involvement in African crises. Has the situation changed? During President Clinton's visit to Kigali in February 1998, he acknowledged U.S. responsibility for failing to prevent the genocide. Initial support for United Nations operations in Sierra Leone and the Democratic Republic of Congo in late 1999 have suggested a new if still insufficient willingness to reengage. For this writer it is clear that these are challenges the United States needs to meet. Moral principles and national self-interest argue forcefully against disengagement from Africa's conflicts. Their consequences, including increased numbers of refugees, arms proliferation, and the spread of AIDS, will inevitably come back to our own doorsteps.

This inquiry seeks to put the tragic events in Sierra Leone in context and to demythologize its postindependence history. Kaplan contends that chaos and violence arose from cultural and sociological failures in African society that were endemic and irreversible, virtually beyond human control. This study argues instead that the sources of Sierra Leone's collapse were political, attributable to specific leaders and their coteries. State collapse is neither irreversible nor destined to remain the fate of Sierra Leone in perpetuity. There is a new generation of Sierra Leoneans who fought successfully for democratic elections in 1996. Many returned home following the reversal of the May 1997 coup or remain prepared to do so. They potentially offer the country opportunities for a new departure from the past. Clearly, the social and economic costs of long-term failure—including the indefinite care of hundreds of thousands of refugees and internally displaced persons—will far exceed the costs of implementing the reconstruction and development programs proposed by the United Nations and the World Bank.

The breakdown of state authority in Sierra Leone and the criminal violence of the Revolutionary United Front during the last decade have often been perceived as internal matters. As with other internal conflicts, however, regional and international players have had a significant role in the downward spiral of civil conflict since 1991, in the flawed efforts at peace negotiations in 1996 and 1999, and in the restoration of the elected government by West African peacekeepers in 1998. I have therefore organized the following four chapters along chronological lines, highlighting the internal and external factors that led to Sierra Leone's collapse. These same factors are relevant to the new challenges posed by the RUF's seizure of United Nations peacekeepers and the envisaged prosecution of Foday Sankoh. The fifth chapter offers an assessment of the international community's role both at the regional level and through the United Nations; a reflection on what more could have been done to avert the present crisis; and a consideration of the broader implications of declining international will and resources for the future of Sierra Leone and other African states emerging from protracted crises.

This inquiry is both a historical overview and a personal commentary drawing on the three years I served as U.S. ambassador in Freetown. While for narrative reasons I have sought in these pages to present events chronologically in a more or less coherent picture, much of what transpired was at the time confused, poorly understood, or simply unknowable. Many of those who influenced the course of the war were outside Sierra Leone or acting covertly. Neither the government nor the resident diplomatic community ever had what could be regarded as the full picture.

In writing this account, I have drawn on my recall and, in a broad sense, from my interaction with government officials, United Nations and other diplomats, and the many Sierra Leoneans whom I had the privilege to meet during my tenure. I trust that these pages will be faithful to their generosity of spirit and intellect in sharing their experiences and insights with me. I also met briefly in the first months of 1996 with representatives of the RUF who were subsequently taken hostage for their efforts to implement the Abidjan Agreement. Following the May 1997 coup, I acted as an informal observer at a number of ECOWAS deliberations in the region and briefings at the United Nations. I am very grateful to all who shared their perspectives with me in those eventful years.

NOTES

1. United Nations Security Council, Secretary-General's Report to the UN Security Council, "The Causes of Conflict and the Promotion of Durable Peace and Sustainable Development in Africa," April 16, 1998; Government of Sweden, Ministry of Foreign Affairs, "Preventing Violent Conflict: A Swedish Action Plan," 1999, p. 24.

2. UN High Commissioner for Human Rights Mary Robinson welcomed the peace accord but responded to the outcry against amnesty by calling for an international inquiry into atrocities committed during the eight-year conflict. Sierra Leone News, "UN Rights Boss Urges Probe of Sierra Leone Abuses," July 10, 1999.

3. Khareen Pech, "Executive Outcomes—A Corporate Conquest," and Ian Douglas, "Fighting for Diamonds: Private Military Companies in Sierra Leone," in Jakkie Cilliers and Peggy Mason (eds.), *Peace Profits or Plunder: The Privatisation of Security in War-Torn African Societies* (Johannesburg, South Africa: Institute for Security Studies, Halfway House, 1999).

4. United Nations, *The Sixth Report of the Secretary-General on the United Nations Mission in Sierra Leone*, August 24, 2000, S/2000/832, called for an increase in troop strength in Sierra Leone up to 20,500.

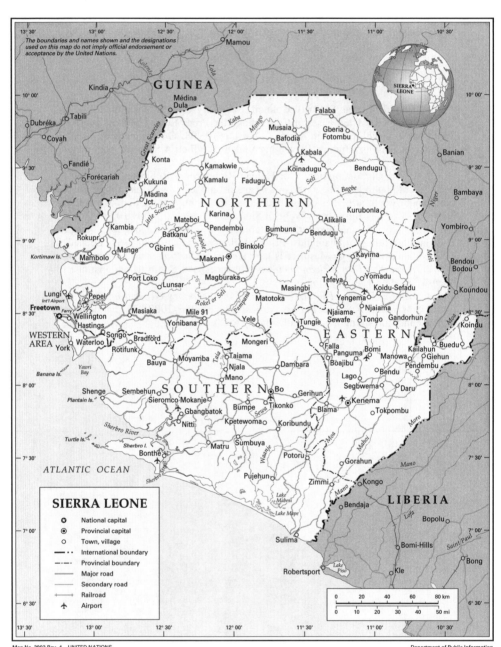

The boundaries and names shown and the designations used on this map do not imply official endorsement or acceptance by the United Nations.

GUINEA

SIERRA LEONE

Mamou

Kindia
Médina Dula
Falaba
Dubréka
Tabili
Musaia
Gberia Fotombu
Coyah
Bafodia
Banian
Fandié
Konta
Kabala
Forécariah
Kamakwie
Koinadugu
Bendugu
Kukuna
Kamalu
Fadugu
Bambaya
Madina Jct.
NORTHERN
Kurubonla
Kambia
Mateboi
Karina
Alikalia
Yombiro
Rokupr
Batkanu
Pendembu
Bumbuna
Bendugu
Kortimaw Is.
Mambolo
Mange
Gbinti
Binkolo
Kayima
Bendou Bodou
Port Loko
Lunsar
Magburaka
Tefeya
Yomadu
Koundou
Lungi
Int'l Airport
Pepel
Masingbi
Koidu-Sefadu
Freetown
Ferry
Matotoka
Yengema
Njaiama
Gandorhun
Wellington
Masiaka
Mile 91
Njaiama-Sewafe
Tongo
Koindu
Hastings
Yonibana
Yele
Tungie
WESTERN AREA
Songo
Bradford
Mongeri
EASTERN
Kailahun
Buedu
York
Waterloo
Rotifunk
Falla
Bomi
Manowa
Giehun
Banana Is.
Yawri Bay
Bauya
Moyamba
Taiama
Panguma
Boajibu
Pendembu
Njala
Dambara
Lago
Bendu
Mano
Segbwema
Daru
Shenge
Sembehun
SOUTHERN
Bo
Gerihun
Plantain Is.
Sieromco Mokanje
Bumpe
Tikonko
Kenema
Tokpombu
Gbangbatok
Blama
Nitti
Kpetewoma
Koribundu
Sherbro River
Matru
Sumbuya
Turtle Is.
Sherbro I.
Bonthe
Potoru
Gorahun
ATLANTIC OCEAN
Pujehun
Zimmi
Kongo
LIBERIA
Bendaja
Bopolu
Lake Mabesi
Lake Mape
Sulima
Bomi-Hills
Bong
Robertsport
Lake Piso
Kle

SIERRA LEONE

⊕ National capital
◉ Provincial capital
○ Town, village
–·–· International boundary
–·–· Provincial boundary
        Major road
        Secondary road
+——+ Railroad
✈ Airport

0   20   40   60   80 km
0 10 20 30 40 50 mi

13° 30'   13° 00'   12° 30'   12° 00'   11° 30'   11° 00'   10° 30'
10° 00'
9° 30'
9° 00'
8° 30'
8° 00'
7° 30'
7° 00'
6° 30'

Map No. 3902 Rev. 4   UNITED NATIONS
December 1999

Department of Public Information
Cartographic Section

1

Origins of the Crisis

The contemporary traveler approaches Freetown from the air and lands at Lungi International Airport, which is separated from the city by the third-largest natural harbor in the world. The flight path follows the Rokel River across clusters of palm trees, brush land, and small villages. The city is out of sight, and the airport appears to be surrounded only by bush. Approaching from the sea, however, the early Portuguese, Dutch, and English navigators all remarked on the extraordinary setting of what became the city of Freetown. A long line of verdant hills overlooking the Atlantic Ocean provides one of the most spectacular natural vistas in the world. In 1462 the Portuguese navigator Pedro da Cintra mapped this mountainous peninsula, marking the entrance to a great harbor that he called Sera Lyoa or Lion Mountain. Legend has it that the name comes from the appearance of the hills in the shape of a lion's mane when viewed from the sea.

THE MODERN CITY

For the modern traveler, only ramshackle vestiges remain as visible reminders of the city's colonial past. Over the thirty-nine years since independence in 1961, the city's infrastructure has progressively deteriorated. Despite the destruction in the city over the past two years, Freetown retains a grungy charm not found elsewhere on the West African coast. The landmarks of the city's history can still be found with a resourceful guide. Near the Customs House is King Jimmy's Wharf where the first British trading ships landed for resupply. Also along the waterfront is the gate through which returned slaves passed, above it a plaque praising Britain's magnanimity. At the city's center next to State House and the American Embassy is the Cotton Tree, where, legend has it, former American slaves offered hymns of thanksgiving for their freedom. Downtown is a combination of British colonial public buildings, nondescript modern banks, and Victorian clapboard houses. One of these is the City Hotel, later a squatter camp, the setting for the opening pages of Graham Greene's novel *The Heart of the Matter*, which he wrote after living in Freetown from 1942 to 1944 while tracking Nazi submarines in the South Atlantic for British intelligence. Remarkably, many wooden structures remain intact after a century or more (even though many others were destroyed in the 1997–1999 fighting). As the violence has abated, the narrow streets are again congested on normal days with traders blocking pedestrian traffic. On the cooler hillsides are the houses of the well to do, including those built by officials who have benefited from recent coups.

ORIGINS: GEOGRAPHY AND PEOPLE

Sierra Leone is a small country, roughly the size of the Republic of Ireland, surrounded by larger neighbors Guinea and Liberia, and bordering the Atlantic Ocean. While independence came to Sierra Leone in 1961, the country's history goes back centuries. Long before the British protectorate of the colonial era, a flourishing multiethnic culture and society had evolved. West Africa was home to numerous waves of migrating peoples traveling from North and East Africa throughout the last two thousand years.[1] Of fourteen ethnic groups that settled in Sierra Leone, three groups—the Mende, Temne, and Limba—were numerically dominant.[2] Successive waves of migration created close cultural ties between peoples falling on different sides of the borders of the nineteenth century. In the north of Sierra Leone where Temnes were in the majority, there have been distinct cultural influences from Guinea, Senegal, and Mali. There was also an influence from the Mandinka (Mandingo) people, the ruling group of the Mali empire who moved into Sierra Leone from the thirteenth to the seventeenth century as Islamic scholars, scribes, and merchants. Sierra Leone was on the periphery of this empire and benefited from the vast trading routes that brought North African and West African influences together. Islam became the dominant religion in the north, although animist traditions have persisted. The traditional importance of the institution of kingship was also stressed, evolving into the contemporary system of paramount chiefs. In the south, where the Mende were dominant, cultural connections are most strong with people in Liberia and Côte d'Ivoire.

The first recorded interaction with Europeans occurred during the Portuguese naval expeditions in the second half of the fifteenth century. Portuguese traders moved up the Rokel River as far as Port Loko and many intermarried, creating a group of Afro-Portuguese who mixed Catholic and African traditions. Their first creole speech became the antecedent of the modern Krio language that in turn, through the slave trade, came to the coastal islands of South Carolina and Georgia as Gullah.

The establishment of Freetown, the "province of freedom," in 1787 as a British post and a settlement for former slaves marks the beginning of the colonial era. The British had been operating out of Bunce Island, one of the largest slave-trading operations on the Gold Coast since around 1750. Afro-English descendants of these slaves dominated the coastal trade and further developed the roots of the Krio language. The Krios, who today constitute only 2 to 3 percent of the population, are descended from former slaves who settled in Freetown between 1787 and 1850 in four waves. The first group were relocated to Freetown when the British Parliament outlawed slavery on British soil in 1787. The second wave came from Nova Scotia, made up of American slaves who had fought for the British during the American Revolution.[3] The third group were the Maroons, slaves who had escaped and lived free in the mountains of Jamaica. The largest wave were the Recaptives, rescued from slave ships stopped by the British navy on the high seas after passage of the Anti-Slavery Act of 1807.[4] From their naval base in Freetown, the British captured slave vessels plying the coast, settling former slaves from across West Africa in and around the growing Freetown colony.

From the early nineteenth century on, the Krios assumed a dominant position relative to the indigenous African population. When Freetown became a Crown Colony in 1808, British administrators, teachers, and missionaries created a large Christian community in that area. The Krios entered the British colonial service, developed schools and businesses, and established the acclaimed Fourah Bay College in 1827. African students from Nigeria, Ghana, and elsewhere attended the college, earning Freetown a wide reputation as the "Athens of West Africa." Krio doctors, teachers, and clergy formed a well-educated class who served British interests through their capable administration of the colonial apparatus.

At the turn of the century, British administration was confined to Freetown and its environs. The British allowed the local chiefs to maintain traditional rule in the hinterland. Through treaties with individual kings and chiefs, the British sought to protect their trade routes until 1896, when Britain declared a "protectorate" over this area. In the period of Anglo-French colonial rivalry, the protectorate served as a barrier against French encroachment through Guinea. In 1898, in one of the earliest manifestations of anticolonial sentiment, Temne leader Bai Bureh led forces from several chiefdoms in the Hut Tax War in protest of British taxation. The Mende in the south also revolted, hitting at trade and Christian missions in the attempt to expel the Europeans.[5] By 1899, the British had reestablished a measure of indirect rule that kept control through the power of hereditary paramount chiefs.

In 1914, the British sought to bind the protectorate economically to the Crown Colony by construction of a railroad linking Freetown to the mining areas of the interior. Trade between the coast and the interior flourished. Traders lived and moved freely between Guinea, Liberia, and Sierra Leone as commerce flowed easily across the Mano River between Sierra Leone and Liberia or by small coastal ships plying between Monrovia, Freetown, and Conakry. When, in 1973, Sierra Leone joined Liberia and Guinea in the Mano River Union, customs and other regulations were eliminated. In practice, however, the three governments have never been able to exercise effective administrative control of their borders. When Liberian factions expanded their deadly fighting into eastern Sierra Leone in 1991, they faced no obstacles to carrying arms, diamonds, and other contraband across the nominal borders. Overall, Liberians, through cultural connections to their "cousins" across the border, were able to travel and communicate with little difficulty until local bands impeded transit by extracting bribes at makeshift checkpoints. The same problem was to plague internal travel within Sierra Leone.

Sierra Leone's history reflects a fundamental paradox: before independence it was, at one level, a remarkable example of peaceful coexistence among peoples of diverse religious beliefs and backgrounds. Fourteen different ethnic groups lived according to Islamic, Christian, and animist traditions. Intermarriage was common and there was little ethnic tension. Yet geographically based ethnic tensions between Mendes in the south and Temnes and Limbas in the north, manipulated by politicians, were to be at the root of the state's progressive collapse in the nearly four decades since independence.

As independence approached, and especially in the first decade of the newly independent nation, relationships between Freetown and the protectorate, and within the protectorate between northerners and southerners, became subject to various kinds of political manipulation. The cleavages operated on two levels. First was the decline of the Krios in the postindependence period. The educated Krios, sometimes described as "Black Settlers," initially occupied a social and economic position analogous to that of the Americo-Liberians in neighboring Liberia or to the white minority in South Africa and Rhodesia. Key nationalists who pressed for independence came from their ranks, and the Krios retained a significant presence in the first postindependence cabinet. But given their small numbers, the Krios soon found themselves politically marginalized, underscored by the sharp decline of their influence in the civil service, the judiciary, and the professional classes. Once elections were held on a one man–one vote basis throughout the country, the Krios also lost representation in the Legislative Assembly. The preindependence Land Tenure Act, which prohibited Krio ownership of land outside of the Crown Colony, further widened the gulf between Krios and other more populous groups. Most professional Krios had very little contact with other Sierra Leoneans of similar background.[6] The second and most fundamental political divide was ethnic and regional. The Mendes, who lived mostly in the south, took over control of the Sierra Leone People's Party (SLPP); the Temnes and Limbas from the north became drawn to the All People's Congress (APC).

DIAMONDS: A MAJOR SOURCE OF CONFLICT

Sierra Leone's misfortune has been geological as well as political. Diamonds were a major factor for the combatants in the cross-border war that has engulfed Sierra Leone for most of the past decade. The Kono region in the east is rich in alluvial diamonds, easily accessible to anyone who can get there with a shovel and sieve. When I visited that area in March 1997, I saw a Bruegel version of hell, with hundreds of young men moving huge piles of dirt from one open pit to another, looking in the tailings, the remnants of ground other miners had already scoured many times. As in Las Vegas, everyone hoped to strike it rich just one time. When I asked a high-ranking official in Freetown the following week whether this was the best way for a young man to spend his time, he replied that it was better than doing nothing or being a rebel cutting off the arms and legs of peasant villagers.

The economic power of the diamond trade has been a major source of conflict in other African countries, most notably Angola, the Democratic Republic of Congo (DRC), and Liberia. Sierra Leone diamonds have financed the rebel movements of both Foday Sankoh and Charles Taylor. Successive mining ministers agreed to provide mining concessions to various foreign entrepreneurs for large bribes, or joined in the mining and smuggling themselves, either openly or as silent partners. In three years, I encountered a steady flow of alleged investors, export-import managers, mining engineers, or outright thieves; they all had their eye on easy pickings. Some of them also found opportunities to engage in the lucrative arms trade as civil chaos and cross-border fighting sputtered on for years. For those who wanted to avoid the small tax imposed by the government on legal diamond exports, the porous border with Liberia constituted an easy alternative. According to one recent estimate, Sierra Leone in the mid-1990s produced $300 million to $450 million worth of diamonds annually, almost all smuggled through Liberia and the Côte d'Ivoire.[7] In all likelihood less than 10 percent of these diamonds passed through the govern-

Diamond prospectors sift through the earth in the
Corbert mine in Waiima, Sierra Leone, 40 kilometers (25 miles)
east of Bo in central Sierra Leone, Wednesday, May 24, 2000.

ment's official channel, the Government Gold and Diamond Office
(GGDO), which collected taxes and duties of 3 percent on assessed value.[8]
The government's revenues from the legal diamond trade in the 1990s have
been negligible.[9]

The origins of this problem go back to the discovery of diamonds in
1930 in Kono. The British colonial government sought to maintain political
stability in the rebellious hinterlands in the face of decreasing financial
support from London. Their solution was twofold: to institute indirect rule
through the traditional paramount chiefs and to use a tributary system
whereby miners received a share of any gold or diamonds they recovered in
lieu of wages. According to William Reno, these dual arrangements progressively degraded the state's control and thwarted the development of
strong legitimate governmental institutions to prevent corruption. The
efforts to control the production and export of diamonds and gold led over
time to what Reno has called the "shadow state."[10] This parallel structure
with no responsibility or accountability to the public ultimately dominated
the minerals sector. Moreover, the larger the sway and extent of the shadow
state, the weaker and poorer the official government apparatus has been.

From the 1930s on, the diamond sector was nominally under the control of successive concessionaires or parastatals. In 1934 the Sierra Leone Selection Trust (SLST), a De Beers subsidiary, was granted a ninety-nine-year monopoly. The SLST promptly generated discord by demanding that outsiders be removed from the mining areas and illicit mining nipped in the bud. The colonial administration granted the paramount chiefs control of settlement and local migration in order to placate the local population. As local chiefs obtained the power to decide who would live in Kono, illicit mining grew apace in the 1940s and 1950s as those with money and connections found ways to circumvent the SLST monopoly. Another important precedent was established in 1936 when the SLST was allowed to field a "security force" of thirty-five armed men to patrol the mining areas. Its role foreshadowed the arrival of Executive Outcomes, Lifeguard, and other private security forces to protect state and private mining resources in the 1990s.

As SLST controls lapsed, the massive entry of Sierra Leoneans into the mining sector had deleterious consequences beyond the patterns of corruption and illicit activity. Local agriculture was severely hurt in the Kono region as many workers were drawn to mining. The unexpected inflow of migrants further undermined the capacity of the chronically underfinanced local administration to address the growing social, economic, and health problems in the area.

In 1955 a group of local miners stormed the SLST security forces and police station, bringing the situation to a head. The colonial administration was forced to give way, reducing the SLST's territory and granting local miners the right to engage in legalized small mining operations. While licensing and tributor arrangements with small miners proceeded, the administration clamped down on foreigners (Lebanese, Guineans, and others), finally forcing forty thousand of them out of Kono.

The establishment of the Mining Area Development Administration (MADA), also in 1955, provided additional resources to develop the region's economic potential as well as to keep it stable for continued mining. In 1962–1963 these funds reportedly were used to buy electoral support as the Kono Progressive Movement (KPM) entered into competition with the ruling SLPP. Thus diamond money and control of the region became interlaced with the broader political agendas of the day. The informal illicit diamond market and those who benefited from it became players in the rivalry between the SLPP and the APC, which had emerged as the major political parties. The Lebanese and other foreigners still residing in Kono were caught in the middle. Often perceived as responsible for corruption, they had in effect no choice but to participate if they were going to continue to operate.[11]

Further degradation of the mining sector continued after independence. The National Diamond Mining Corporation (NDMC) started as a joint government-SLST venture in 1970. The directors drew down their assets with the construction of expensive housing as well as large salaries and other emoluments. When the SLST pulled out in 1984, the official diamond sector was clearly failing. The state had lost control of its assets, enabling private entrepreneurs to take over Kono and adjacent diamond-rich regions. From the 1930s to the present, diamonds became the crucial keystone in the widespread pattern of corruption and private benefit that has remained beyond the institutional capacity of successive governments to control. Ultimately the patterns of the 1930s–1960s set the stage for the events of the 1990s.[12]

SIERRA LEONE SINCE INDEPENDENCE

Sierra Leone's troubled history reflects a familiar pattern in postindependence Africa: a brief experiment in democracy in the early 1960s quickly replaced by thirty years of one-party civilian government or military rule. A dismal pattern of official corruption, mismanagement, and electoral violence led over the years to deepening public cynicism, the virtual collapse of the education system, and the creation of a generation of young men and women who became the Revolutionary United Front's (RUF) rank and file.[13] This did not have to happen. The country's first prime minister, Sir Milton Margai—head of the Sierra Leone People's Party (SLPP)—though he changed little of what the British had established, was much beloved and genuinely sought to build a unified nation. Upon Sir Milton's death in 1964, the pattern of corrupt politics began and accelerated as the leadership passed to his brother Albert, who by all accounts saw the state not as a stewardship in the public interest but as the power base for personal gain and aggrandizement.

Regional and ethnic factors also came into play early on. Albert's use of patronage led the SLPP to become an ever more ethnic party, drawing its support primarily from the Mende networks in the south and east, to which he directed the spoils of political power. The APC quickly attracted the support of the Temnes and Limbas of the north as well as other smaller ethnic groups (Loko, Mandingo, Susu, etc.). At its helm was Siaka Stevens, a wily politician who quickly developed the ability to dominate Sierra Leone's politics through a combination of guile, flattery, bribery, and intimidation. At the outset, however, Stevens presented a legitimate challenge to the ruling party. Stevens won the 1967 election, the first time in postindependence Africa that an opposition leader defeated a prime minister. Margai, unwilling to relinquish power, sought to reverse the popular decision, first through a parliamentary maneuver and then by encouraging a military coup. After a quick spurt of coups and countercoups in 1967, Stevens was finally sworn in as the democratically elected president in 1968. As one observer has concluded, "Albert Margai's attempt to subvert the multi-democratic constitution, and the intervention of the military in 1967, paved the way for what became a military nightmare in the nineties."[14]

Siaka Stevens's rule (1968–1985) met all the criteria of "Big Man" African politics. Stevens was a master of manipulation, of the velvet glove sometimes turned to iron, of Tammany Hall politics African style.[15] Stevens came into office as the prime minister in a multiparty political system built on the British model and stepped down seventeen years later as president of a one-party state. When co-optation did not work, he resorted to trumped-up treason charges and executed some of his rivals. When all else failed, he called in Guinean troops to quell an incipient army uprising in 1973.[16] As his aspirations for pan-African recognition soared, he bankrupted the treasury to perpetuate his rule. In 1980 he undertook mammoth, expensive infrastructure projects, including the construction of the Bintumani Hotel and a residential complex to host the Organization of African Unity (OAU) summit. Stevens was duly elected OAU chairman but the hotel and the village promptly fell into disrepair while the newly installed streetlights flickered out barely six weeks later. Wildly inflated contracts enabled those who were insiders on the scam to walk away with millions.

Stevens's rule was called the "seventeen-year plague of locusts." He destroyed and corrupted every institution of the state. Parliament was gutted of significance; judges were intimidated or bribed; the university was starved of funds; many professors compromised their integrity by joining the cabinet; the value of education itself was deprecated in favor of the quick acquisition of wealth; and the professionalism of the army was undermined. Those who opposed the imposition of the one-party state in 1977 were either executed, forced into exile, or reduced to a condition of penury. Bank of Sierra Leone governor Sam L. Bangura was killed under mysterious circumstances in 1979 after challenging the wisdom of lavish expenditures on the OAU summit.[17]

In assessing how all this could happen, it has been noted that there were courageous men who stood up to Stevens. But many of those who were ultimately drawn into the net were either weak, rapacious, or unprincipled. Resident diplomats did not raise a hue and cry about these developments, which were regarded as internal problems of little consequence to the economic interests of the British, Americans, or others. None of them could anticipate the longer-term consequences. Moreover, as these were matters of local politics, they had little or no international resonance.

FROM STEVENS TO MOMOH: THE CONTINUING SLIDE

Stevens stepped down in 1985, turning the reins of power over to his chosen successor, Major General Joseph Momoh, whose only claim on the
nation's top position was his sycophantic and fawning loyalty to his leader.
Momoh was notoriously inept. When he assumed office the public expected
a new leadership. They became quickly disillusioned when Momoh's early
cabinet was made up of recycled APC politicians. Stevens continued to be
influential behind the scenes, maintaining contact with his corrupt friends
and former colleagues. Two years later, Stevens, who apparently still had
political ambitions, together with two high-level accomplices, plotted
Momoh's assassination.[18] The coup was discovered before it could be carried out. Momoh placed Stevens under house arrest and he died estranged
from his family several months later. Stevens was given a state funeral but
his gravesite stands strangely unmarked next to the elaborately lapidary
tombstone of the country's first leader, Sir Milton Margai. Even free of his
old leader, Momoh proved unable to exercise effective leadership.

In retrospect, his seven-year tenure is remembered as the period of the
country's economic collapse and disastrous involvement in the evolving
Liberian civil war. Unchecked corruption and poor fiscal management led
in short order to the government's bankruptcy. Unpaid civil servants des-
perate to keep their families fed ransacked their offices, stealing furniture,
typewriters, and light fixtures. In the capital, electricity, gasoline, and cur-
rency were extremely scarce. One observer has noted that the government
hit bottom when it stopped paying schoolteachers and the education system
collapsed. Without their salaries, teachers sought fees from the parents to
prepare children for their exams. With only professional families able to
pay these fees, many children ended up on the streets without either education or economic opportunity. The alienated and despairing youth who
fought with the RUF or were to be seen aimlessly roaming the streets of the
capital in the mid-1990s were the product of this situation.[19]

The pattern of corruption and misrule set by Stevens and Momoh had
an impact that went far beyond those who immediately stood to gain (or
lose) by manipulation of government funds, smuggling of diamonds, or
poaching of the lucrative fishing grounds. As infrastructure and public
ethics deteriorated in tandem, much of the professional class left the country, using their family connections and money to emigrate to Europe and
the United States. The thousands of Sierra Leoneans who went abroad in
the 1970s and 1980s left behind a country sliding inexorably to the bottom.
According to United Nations statistics, by the early 1990s, Sierra Leone
ranked among the poorest countries of the world notwithstanding ample
natural resources including diamonds, gold, bauxite, rutile, iron ore, marine
life, coffee, and cocoa. As President Kabbah said in a rueful thirty-seventh-

anniversary independence speech on April 27, 1998, Sierra Leone at independence ranked ahead of Malaysia and Singapore only to find itself almost four decades later ranked below even Somalia and Rwanda.

CROSS-BORDER WAR: FROM LIBERIA TO SIERRA LEONE

On March 23, 1991, a group of about a hundred fighters including Sierra Leonean dissidents, Liberian fighters loyal to Charles Taylor, and a small number of mercenaries from Burkina Faso invaded eastern Sierra Leone at Bomaru, Kailahun District. A second flank was opened in Pujehun District to the southwest. In early April, a communiqué appeared announcing that the rebellion had been started by the Revolutionary United Front (RUF) led by an ex-Sierra Leone army corporal and professional photographer named Foday Sankoh. The RUF set forth a vaguely populist agenda of fighting against government officials and their business associates in Freetown who had plundered the country's resources.[20] In practice, their wrath was to be directed against the rural peasantry, the group least responsible for or able to influence the actions of those in control in Freetown.

It was the start of what turned out to be, with interruptions, has a decade long cross-border and civil war that was to progressively engulf the entire country. It is useful to recall briefly how Sankoh and Charles Taylor met and entered into the collaborative relationship that has had such a profoundly destructive impact on Sierra Leone and the region. Sankoh had participated in a failed 1971 coup attempt against Siaka Stevens, for which he was confined to Pademba Road Prison (where he was to return in 1998) for most of the 1970s and given a dishonorable discharge from the army.[21] When he was released, Sankoh returned briefly to Segbwema, where he set up shop as a commercial photographer. Sankoh was an admirer of Patrice Lumumba, Muammar Qaddafi, Thomas Sankara of Burkina Faso, and Jerry Rawlings of Ghana, all of whom he saw as populist anti-Western leaders. Sometime in the 1980s, he headed for Libya where he met another neighboring contender for power—Liberian warlord and now president, Charles Taylor. They became adherents of Qaddafi's crusade against weak pro-Western regimes including those in Sierra Leone and Liberia. Qaddafi provided both men and their followers a potent cocktail of anti-imperialist rhetoric, guerrilla training, arms, and money.

While Sankoh had his grievances against the Momoh regime, he probably would not have gotten far without the collaboration of Taylor and support from Libya. Thus, the Sierra Leonean and Liberian crises were intertwined from the outset. Throughout the 1980s, Liberia was convulsed by civil war as a number of competing factions sought to depose Samuel Doe, an army sergeant who in 1980 had seized power in a brutal coup against the

Americo-Liberian government headed by <u>William Tolbert.</u> Over the ensuing decade the U.S. government provided over $500 million to the Doe regime. Liberia was an asset in the Cold War struggle to reduce Soviet influence, giving Americans access to Roberts International Airport and permitting the establishment of a major communications network in Africa. The Americans convinced themselves that with substantial economic support they could somehow make Doe into a responsible, if not necessarily democratic, leader. Doe's main factional opponent was Charles Taylor's National Patriotic Front of Liberia (NPFL). Taylor's complex career included conviction for embezzlement in his role as head of a government procurement agency. He fled Liberia for the United States, where he was arrested only to escape from the Massachusetts prison to avoid extradition to Liberia and certain execution by the Doe regime. When the Independent NPFL, a breakaway faction led by Prince Johnson, captured Doe in 1989, he was brutally executed, an event recorded for posterity on videotape.

The NPFL was to prove itself the most powerful and effective of the Liberian factions. In the early 1990s, however, it found itself under siege by the newly formed Economic Community of West African States Cease-Fire Monitoring Group (ECOMOG).[22] When President Momoh allowed ECOMOG to use Lungi as an assembly point and airbase, and dispatched Sierra Leone Army (SLA) forces to join other ECOMOG units in Liberia, Taylor retaliated by providing arms and ammunition to Sankoh's RUF fighters in their combat against the Freetown regime. While some SLA officers and soldiers fought to defeat the RUF, from the outset many entered into collaboration with the rebels, earning them the sobriquet *sobels*, that is, soldiers by day, rebels by night. The RUF attacked economic targets in the south, putting the Momoh regime under considerable pressure.

Sankoh's effort to bring down the Momoh government goes back to the 1971 coup attempt against Stevens and his resentment against the harsh treatment meted out to the coup plotters.[23] But it was the Sierra Leone army junior officers' discontent with their conditions of service that led to Momoh's downfall. As Liberia descended into its long nightmare, Captains Valentine Strasser and Julius Maada Bio and others were part of the Sierra Leonean contingent fighting in Monrovia under ECOMOG command against Taylor's NPFL. Momoh subsequently sent them in 1991 to Kailahun and Kenema to fight the RUF rebels. When the government failed to pay their salaries or provide medical treatment for their wounded, the junior officers staged a protest on April 29, 1992, at State House. Momoh thought he was facing a violent coup and fled ignominiously to Guinea.[24] Little could he know that his two successors would later on occupy the same villa in Conakry also as the guests of Guinea's president Lansana Conté.

NOTES

1. Talabi Lucan's *A Visual History of West Africa* (Nigeria: Evans Brothers, 1981) provides an in-depth history of the waves of migration, the trading routes, and early kingdoms in West Africa. *Africa South of the Sahara 2000* (London: Europa, 1999) provides useful background information. Peter K. Mitchell, "Sierra Leone: Physical and Social Geography," in *Africa South of the Sahara 2000*, p. 95.

2. The major groups are Mendes (32 percent), Temnes (31 percent), and Limbas (8 percent). In Joseph Opala, "Sierra Leone, The Politics of State Collapse," unpublished manuscript, Conference on "Irregular Warfare in Liberia and Sierra Leone," SAIC, Denver, CO, July 30–August 1, 1998.

3. James Brooke, "For Nova Scotia Blacks, Veil Is Ripped From Past," *New York Times*, October 8, 1999.

4. See Joseph Opala, "The People of Sierra Leone," *Sierra Leone: International Crisis Group Report to the Japanese Government* (Brussels: ICG, April 1996), for a detailed description of linguistic and ethnic groups in Sierra Leone.

5. Opala, "The People of Sierra Leone"; Christopher Clapham, "Recent History of Sierra Leone," in *Africa South of the Sahara 2000* (London: Europa, 1999), pp. 951–954.

6. Syl Cheney-Coker, "Agony of a State," unpublished manuscript, September 1999.

7. As estimated by Caspar Fithen, a specialist on Africa and diamonds at Oxford Analytica, quoted in James Rupert, "Diamond Hunters Fuel Africa's Brutal Wars," *The Washington Post*, October 16, 1999.

8. Ibid.

9. See Ian Smillie, Lansana Gberie, and Ralph Hazelton, *The Heart of the Matter: Sierra Leone, Diamonds, and Human Security* (Toronto: Partnership Africa Canada, 2000), pp. 38–47, for an in-depth account of the origins and operations of the diamond industry in Sierra Leone.

10. See William Reno, *Corruption and State Politics in Sierra Leone* (Cambridge: Cambridge University Press, 1995) for an analysis of the key role of diamonds in the emergence of the "shadow state."

11. Smillie et al., *The Heart of the Matter,* pp. 38–43.

12. Ibid.

13. Paul Richards, "Rebellion in Liberia and Sierra Leone: A Crisis of Youth?" in O. W. Furley (ed.), *Conflict in Africa* (London: Tauris, 1995).

14. Cheney-Coker, "Agony of a State."

15. Tammany Hall was the popular name for the Democratic political machine based on corruption in New York City during the 1800s. Tammany bosses including William M. Tweed ruled the city for almost a century. "Boss" Tweed controlled nominations and patronage in New York City Democratic politics after 1857. The Tweed Ring, which consisted of Tweed, the mayor, the city comptroller, and the city chamberlain, sold political favors and defrauded the city of at least $30 million during that time.

16. Fred Hayward, "Sierra Leone: State Consolidation, Fragmentation, and Decay," in C. O'Brien, L. Cruise, R. Rathbone, and J. Dunn (eds.), *Contemporary West African States* (Cambridge: Cambridge University Press, 1989).

17. See Abdul K. Koroma, *Sierra Leone: The Agony of a Nation* (United Kingdom: Andromeda Publications, 1996), p. 38.

18. Opala, "The People of Sierra Leone."

19. See Revolutionary United Front, "Footpath to Democracy," unpublished manuscript; Opala, "The People of Sierra Leone," pp. 9–12.

20. *Africa Confidential*, "Chronology of Sierra Leone from 1991 to 1998: How Diamonds Fueled the Conflict." http://www.africa-confidential.com/sandline. html, December 6, 1998: Revolutionary United Front, "Lasting Peace in Sierra Leone: the Revolutionary United Front Sierra Leone (RUF/SL) Perspective and Vision."

21. See Koroma, *Sierra Leone*, p. 143, for an account of Sankoh's imprisonment and subsequent career. The exact duration of Sankoh's incarceration is unclear. In a BBC interview in January 2000 he claimed that he had been imprisoned for six years. Koroma, an APC minister, asserts that Sankoh was imprisoned for seven years.

22. Robert Mortimer, "From ECOMOG to ECOMOG II: Intervention in Sierra Leone," in John W. Harbeson and Donald Rothchild (eds.), *Africa in World Politics: The African State System in Flux*, 3d edition (Boulder, CO: Westview Press, 2000). Mortimer provides an excellent account of the transnational Liberian/Sierra Leonean conflicts and the evolving role of ECOMOG in both countries.

23. The abortive coup led to the execution of Army Force Commander John Bangura, Momoh's predecessor, as well as Sankoh's incarceration. Sankoh had an "abiding hatred" of Momoh from then on. See Koroma, *Sierra Leone*, p. 143.

24. In October 1998 Momoh was convicted of treason and sentenced to death for complicity in the May 1997 overthrow of the Kabbah government. The sentence was not carried out. Momoh and others escaped from prison when the RUF reentered Freetown in January 1999.

2

From Military Rule
to the 1996 Elections

Momoh's successor, twenty-seven-year-old Captain Valentine Strasser, was chosen by his army comrades, apparently against his wishes, as the most presentable officer to head the National Provisional Ruling Council (NPRC). The inner group of junior officers believed they could quickly turn the country's dire military and economic situation around and redress popular grievances against the corrupt Momoh government.[1] A sycophantic journalist, Hilton Fyle, made a documentary called *Nightmare in Paradise* in which Strasser, in battle dress and dark RayBan sunglasses, sat behind his desk at State House promising a decisive victory over the Revolutionary United Front (RUF), an end to corruption, improved living standards, and an early restoration of civilian rule.[2] Initial popular support and the readiness of the international community to provide financial assistance through the International Monetary Fund (IMF) and World Bank led to a false sense of overconfidence. The cycle of expectation and disappointment replayed itself: the public's high hopes in a new government were followed by rapid and bitter disillusionment. The NPRC's youth and inexperience (all of the inner circle were in their late twenties or early thirties) led to many mistakes and abuses. But these same factors also subsequently enabled them to agree to relinquish power peacefully provided their personal futures could be organized.

The junior officers initially presented themselves to the public as standard bearers of honest government and transparent administration. The government charged thirty officials in Momoh's government with abuse of office, placed them under house arrest, and confiscated their properties.[3] Three Commissions of Inquiry were established to investigate responsibility for "corruption, mismanagement and misappropriation of public funds so that appropriate punishment can be prescribed for their crimes."[4] On December 29, 1992, while the commissions were in recess, the NPRC carried out extrajudicial executions of twenty-six people whom they accused

35

of plotting against the regime. (When the Armed Forces Revolutionary Council/RUF seized power five years later, they also carried out swift extrajudicial executions of soldiers whom they accused of looting.)[5] The commission proceedings were abruptly terminated, leaving a number of Momoh officials unable to present their defense.[6] The international outcry, however, prompted Strasser again to change course. On the first anniversary of the coup he released over a hundred political prisoners from Pademba Road Prison.

Strasser and his NPRC colleagues had inherited a disastrous military situation. The RUF was in control of the easternmost province of Kailahun, which became its long-term base of operations. The diamond-rich Kono region had fallen to the rebels in late 1992 and been partially brought back under government control in January 1993 only with the assistance of Nigerian troops. When Strasser called a unilateral cease-fire in December 1993, the rebels took advantage of the pause in the fighting to adopt new tactics, splitting up into small commando units targeting civilians and other soft nonmilitary targets in remote rural areas. Vital economic road links between Freetown and the hinterland became death traps as civilian and military targets were ambushed at random. These tactics were to persist throughout the next four years.

The NPRC inherited an army structure demoralized by Siaka Stevens's years of favoritism and disregard for professionalism.[7] The army's standards had declined significantly under Momoh. Until the late 1980s the Sierra Leone army had been largely ceremonial. Momoh had increased its ranks to about three thousand officers and soldiers to fight against the RUF alongside Nigerian and Guinean units. When the NPRC recognized that this was still inadequate, they released prisoners from the jails and dragooned unemployed and uneducated youth from the streets to bolster their numbers. The army's strength officially reached 17,000 by the time the NPRC relinquished office four years later. Actually, no one knew how many soldiers there were, as many of them did not live in camps and there was no organized accounting or census system. Morale was already low and deteriorated further as senior officers diverted rice rations intended for the troops in the field to the commercial markets in Freetown and other cities. Many soldiers found that they could do better by joining with the rebels in looting civilians in the countryside than by fighting against them. By mid-1993 the two sides became virtually indistinguishable. The NPRC's denials of this complicity simply undermined its credibility. As was to become ever more evident, a major factor in the war's prolongation was this collusion between the army and the RUF.

By 1993, the taking of international and Sierra Leonean hostages marked an ominous new trend in the conduct of the war. In November 1994 the RUF captured two British volunteers working on rural development projects in Kabala along with a large number of Sierra Leoneans. In January 1995 the RUF attacked Kambia, close to the border with Guinea, seizing seven nuns who were helping a polio-eradication project. When the RUF reached Wellington on the outskirts of Freetown the same month, there was widespread fear in the capital that the rebels would enter the city and topple the regime. The army offered enough resistance to hold its ground, but the low-intensity guerrilla conflict continued.

As the war dragged on in the south and east, the economy plummeted. The low point came on January 17–18, 1995, when RUF and dissident army elements attacked the Sierromco aluminum and Sierra Rutile mines in the southwest, overrunning both sites within seventy-two hours. The RUF again took foreign and Sierra Leonean hostages (including Dr. Mohamed Barrie, the Sierra Rutile company's physician, who later became an adviser to Foday Sankoh during the 1996 negotiations in Abidjan).[8] At the rutile mine the rebels broke open the safe-deposit vault, emptying it of cash and medicines, while leaving it to the army several days later to loot the residences of the general manager and the expatriate staff. They were notably careful not to destroy the dredges, pontoons, and other major equipment that were intact, if rusty, when the company's overseas managers returned to the site several years later. At one blow the NPRC had lost its principal foreign-exchange earners while being confronted by a tenacious rebel advance.

The strategy of hostage taking began to bring results. After several years in the bush, the RUF attained one of its major objectives: international attention and involvement. The United Nations, the Organization of African Unity (OAU), and the Commonwealth appealed for the release of the hostages.[9] Sankoh asked for International Committee of the Red Cross (ICRC) mediation, demanding the withdrawal of all foreign forces and foreign businessmen, an end to all arms supplies to the government, and the provision of various communication equipment and medical supplies to the RUF. In late March 1996, without these conditions being met, the nuns were released. One month later sixteen of the hostages from the mining sites (ten expatriates and six Sierra Leoneans) as well as the British volunteers were released to the ICRC. The RUF had learned how to obtain publicity if not esteem, a tactic that it continued to pursue over the next three years.[10]

ENTER EXECUTIVE OUTCOMES

The NPRC's efforts to block the RUF's military advance changed fundamentally with the entry of Executive Outcomes (EO) into the equation in April 1995. Executive Outcomes was to win great favor among many

Sierra Leoneans who perceived it as the only force able to stop the RUF.[11] Executive Outcomes was already established as an effective private South African company that had supplied "security specialists," that is, private security forces, to the Angolan government in its fight against the National Union for the Total Independence of Angola. But Executive Outcomes' own origins were highly controversial. In the early 1990s Eeben Barlow, a former officer of the South African Defense Forces, recruited about two thousand men who had served the apartheid regime's military and intelligence services against the African National Congress (ANC) and other antiapartheid elements. These included members of the notorious Koevoet Battalion, which had fought against the South West African People's Organization during the independence struggle in Namibia, and the Civil Coordination Bureau, which had carried out covert assassinations of ANC and other antiapartheid activists. Despite their harsh track record and Nelson Mandela's condemnation of mercenaries, Executive Outcomes was clearly seen as useful to the leaders of Angola and Sierra Leone, both weak states whose armies could not stop rebel onslaughts, and who had nowhere else to turn.[12] Strasser sought help from Executive Outcomes as the RUF advance was within twenty miles of the capital. He later claimed that he read about their role in Angola in *Newsweek* magazine. Executive Outcomes' arrival in Sierra Leone followed the failure and departure of another private security force made up of Nepalese Ghurkas who had been part of the British army. In 1993–1994 the Ghurka Security Group had been providing training to the Sierra Leone army but it was forced to withdraw after suffering heavy losses, including the murder of its American commander, Robert Mackenzie, in an RUF ambush in early 1995.[13]

Diamond mining concessions apparently came into the picture from the start, although there is no documented evidence that this was part of Executive Outcomes' contract with the NPRC. Although they were nominally separate operations, Executive Outcomes was linked through its directorates with Branch Energy Ltd., a relatively new actor in Sierra Leone's lucrative diamond industry. The company's principal stakeholders included British financier Michael Grunwald and former British intelligence operative Tony Buckingham, both of whom were reportedly instrumental in negotiating EO's entry into Sierra Leone.[14] According to Alan Paterson, Branch Energy's managing director, the company invested $12 million in exploration in 1994–1996, a time when most major mining companies had pulled out of Sierra Leone. Most of that expansion, however, followed the arrival of Executive Outcomes.

The initial April 1995 contract between the NPRC and Executive Outcomes provided that, in exchange for military support and advice to the Sierra Leone army, Executive Outcomes was to be paid $1.8 million a month. Strasser contended that a triangular profit-sharing arrangement involved Branch Energy's kimberlite diamond-mining operations in the Kono region. Indeed, the government decree that granted the Kono concession to Branch Energy (three months after Executive Outcomes' arrival in country) gave 5 percent of the value of all diamonds extracted and 37.5 percent of net profits to the government.[15] It was, in Strasser's view, the best arrangement that any foreign company had ever given to Sierra Leone.[16] All this, however, was well in the future, as any large-scale mining operation would require establishment of long-term security.

The army and Executive Outcomes set four immediate objectives: to secure Freetown, to retake the Sierra Rutile mines, to destroy RUF headquarters, and to clear remaining areas under RUF control. Ultimately they attained only the first two of these goals. Although Executive Outcomes' presence was small—about ten Afrikaner officers and two hundred soldiers, mostly of Cape colored origin—they had the military advantage of air capability and the psychological advantage of being an outside force with a fierce reputation for swift and effective action. Early gains on the ground quickly created the near mythological view that Executive Outcomes was invincible. In carrying out these operations, Executive Outcomes entered into an informal relationship with the southern-based rural civilian militias, the Kamajohs, who were to have a major impact on the military balance over the next four years. (Their leader, Chief Sam Hinga Norman, subsequently became Kabbah's deputy defense minister.)[17] Using an MI-8 helicopter to find RUF bases and provide tactical guidance to army ground forces, Executive Outcomes successfully attacked a number of RUF field locations. They quickly pushed RUF forces away from the Freetown area. In December 1995 they retook the Sierra Rutile mine (although security, financial, and logistical problems continued to block the renewal of operations), and in January 1996 they defeated RUF forces in the Kangari Hills, about a hundred kilometers northwest of Freetown. Although they were unable to capture RUF headquarters in Kailahun, their pressure was probably instrumental in the RUF's decision to enter into negotiations with the government after almost five years of fighting.[18]

As Executive Outcomes' operating expenses piled up and Branch Energy was unable to start its mining operations due to the uncertain security situation in the Kono region (the logistical requirements of a large upcountry operation would involve a minimum six-month start-up phase), Executive Outcomes pressed the NPRC to be paid for its services. By December 1995, three months before it was due to leave office, the NPRC was badly in arrears. Shortly before Christmas, Executive Outcomes threatened to withdraw from Sierra Leone unless the arrears were paid. Underscoring their interlocking connections, several Branch Energy officials flew to Freetown for negotiations and a partial payment was made.

Where did the money for these payments come from? The situation is murky. At the end of 1995 there was virtually no formal economic activity in the country. Customs duties and tax collection were negligible. The financially strapped NPRC was heavily dependent on budgetary support from the IMF. While monetary transactions are hard to track down, it seems probable that at least some of the IMF funds deposited in the government's bank accounts may have been used for these payments. In any case, by the time the Kabbah government came into office in late March 1996, Executive Outcomes was reportedly still owed $17 million. The Finance Ministry tried unsuccessfully to renegotiate its payment schedule, and then decided unilaterally to reduce its monthly payments to $1.2 million in order to limit their budgetary impact. In January 1997, President Kabbah—beset by IMF and international donor demands for reduced public expenditures—ordered Executive Outcomes to pack up and leave.[19] Even though a peace agreement had been signed in Abidjan in November 1996, Executive Outcomes' departure before the establishment of a Neutral Monitoring Group intended to monitor breaches of the cease-fire (Article 12) proved a fatal mistake. The RUF renewed its operations in the north. Without the intelligence and tactical capacity of Executive Outcomes to guide him, President Kabbah was to find himself outmaneuvered as preparations by disgruntled army officers continued for another coup attempt.

CIVIL SOCIETY AND BINTUMANI I

In the midst of war, economic collapse, and massive dislocation (at least a quarter of Sierra Leone's population were internally displaced or were refugees in neighboring Guinea and Liberia), an embryonic civil society movement developed. While the NPRC was reluctant to relinquish power, Strasser had made a public commitment early on to do so. A coalition of citizen groups pressed for holding general elections even though the war was continuing. The women's movement took the leading role in this campaign, joined by trade unionists, journalists, local council leaders, paramount chiefs, and well-known academics. The appointment in March 1995 of James Jonah, recently retired as United Nations Under-Secretary-General, as chairman of the Interim National Electoral Commission encouraged these groups to proceed. Among those who were to play major roles were Shirley Gbujama, who became chairperson of the Bintumani Conference and later foreign minister; Zainab Bangura, later head of the Campaign for Good Governance; and Julius Spencer, editor of the crusading *New Breed* newspaper, later minister of information under the third Kabbah government. In the women's movement, key leaders included Yasmin Fofanah and Isha Dyfan, two fearless attorneys, and Amy Smythe, later to become the first minister of women's and children's affairs.

From August 15 to 19, 1995, seventy-five civil society and political representatives met at the Bintumani Conference Center on the Aberdeen peninsula, the behemoth that Siaka Stevens had bequeathed the nation fifteen years earlier, to decide when and how to proceed to elections. A large majority of those assembled pressed for elections by the end of the year. Jonah persuaded the assembly that the elections should be set for March 1996, arguing that time was needed for funds to be mobilized, voter rolls to be prepared, and candidates to present themselves in accordance with the 1991 Constitution.

The minority view at the conference held that it was premature to hold elections while the war against the RUF continued. The slogan of those who urged deferring a decision was "peace before elections." There was a certain logic to their argument that many people would be unable to participate as long as the fighting was going on. However, in reality "peace before elections" was the slogan of those who had an interest in continuation of the war and were doing well under military rule. Its acceptance would have meant either prolongation of the NPRC regime or, as had been suggested, formation of a nonelected transitional government until such time as a peace agreement could be concluded. In effect, Sankoh and his supporters would have been in a position to decide the timing of the election. Although the RUF had been invited to send a representative to the conference, no one attended. Instead, Sankoh made it clear that RUF forces would do all they could to prevent the election from taking place until their demands were met.

THE INTERNAL NPRC COUP

Before the election could take place, an internal drama played itself out within the NPRC. Strasser and his colleagues had a falling-out, divided over whether to allow the election to proceed as scheduled, and concerned over their individual exit strategies. One of the immediate precipitating events took place at the Commonwealth Summit at Auckland, New Zealand, in November 1995. The Commonwealth voted to suspend Nigeria's membership, given its brutal human rights record under Abacha. Strasser would have been hard-pressed to take a different position in front of other heads of states, but the action ill-suited an NPRC that was heavily dependent on the Nigerian forces for their personal security. The second event was Strasser's decision upon his return from New Zealand, reportedly upon the urging of his mother, to present himself as a candidate for the presidency even though he was constitutionally ineligible. The 1991 Constitution required the president to be at least forty years old; Strasser was barely thirty. When Strasser threatened to fire his colleagues if they did not support him, they took action first. On January 16, 1996, barely six weeks before the election—slated for February 26—Strasser was briskly ousted in a peaceful internal coup. During a meeting at Cockerill Defense Headquarters his colleagues quickly surrounded him and put him in hand-cuffs on a waiting helicopter for the thirty-minute flight to Conakry. They had to return later with the key to remove the handcuffs, and to give him his clothing. Strasser became head of state number three to occupy the villa in Conakry. The new NPRC chairman, Julius Maada Bio, told the UK and U.S. ambassadors in terse conversations that he had taken over, that Strasser was safely out of the country, and that elections would take place as scheduled.

NEGOTIATIONS WITH THE RUF

Brigadier General Julius Maada Bio, at age thirty-two, was Strasser's con-temporary but a person of radically different temperament and background. Where Strasser was uncomfortable in public appearances, Maada Bio was self-assured, exuded confidence, and carried himself as a paramount chief in uniform. He came from a "ruling house" in the south and appeared to be intent on having a future for himself beyond the duration of the NPRC. While all previous efforts to engage the RUF in direct negotiations had failed, Maada Bio was determined to give it another try and to get the credit for ending the rebel war. Whether it was prearranged or a genuine new ini-tiative, Maada Bio persuaded Sankoh through radio communications to send a delegation to Abidjan in late February on the eve of the Sierra Leone elections for an initial NPRC-RUF dialogue on establishing a peace process.[20]

Ivorian foreign minister Amara Essy acted as host with UN Special Envoy Berhanu Dinka as well as representatives of the OAU and the Commonwealth in attendance. In mid-March, Sankoh left Sierra Leone for the first time since the war had begun five years earlier. Maada Bio and Sankoh met face to face in Yamoussoukro on March 25, five days before the formal transfer of power to president-elect Ahmed Tejan Kabbah. Officially, the talks concluded with an agreement in principle for the Kabbah government and the RUF to continue negotiations. This in itself was a change in the RUF's position as Sankoh had steadfastly refused to negotiate with any of the Freetown governments, whom he claimed were responsible for plundering the nation's resources in collusion with foreign business interests. Behind the scenes, however, these talks revolved around future power-sharing arrangements. Maada Bio's representatives apparently had implied or promised that they would make Sankoh deputy chairman of the NPRC if the election was canceled or postponed, or use their influence to assure him the vice presidency of a civilian government.[21] Maada Bio was thus apparently either plotting to put off the election or making a commitment he could not keep, but the consequences were to be felt later when negotiations bogged down over Sankoh's insistence that he had been promised the vice presidency. Sankoh also agreed to stay in Abidjan with a small circle of advisers (see Chapter 3), and lived for almost a year thereafter either in the Hotel Ivoire or an adjacent villa as the guest of the Ivorian government. It was to be one of the turning points of the conflict, but not part of a straightforward path to peace as the citizens of Sierra Leone had hoped.

BINTUMANI II

In mid-February, as these exploratory discussions got under way, the NPRC made soundings as to whether the public would accept postponement of the elections. Staged rallies were held in the north and east in order to drum up support for the "peace before elections" campaign. Maada Bio insisted on reconvening the representatives of civil society, and they met again (at Bintumani II) on February 16. This time the atmosphere was tense and uncertain. Armed soldiers stood at Aberdeen Bridge, blocking traffic in order to discourage participants from proceeding to the conference hall in the Bintumani Hotel. One presidential candidate, Thaimu Bangura of the People's Democratic Party, was forcibly pulled out of his car and assaulted, requiring him to be taken to the hospital for emergency treatment. Maada Bio's speech called for law and order and barely referred to the election. Jonah responded with a passionate assertion that he was prepared to be killed, but the forces of democracy would win. His remarks electrified the audience, many of whom were aware that his residence had been firebombed two nights earlier. When the roll call began, Chairman Shirley Gbujama ruled against bloc voting, and prevented anyone not in attendance at Bintumani I from participating. The overwhelming 58 to 17 vote at the end of six hours of deliberations made clear that the participants wanted the elections to proceed.

Pressure to postpone or cancel the elections also came from the RUF, which was carrying out a series of hit-and-run attacks on villages in the north and east. The RUF sought to persuade people to boycott the election, and they acted with great brutality and contempt for human life. They adopted a deliberate policy of mutilations and amputations of helpless civilians, indiscriminately chopping off hands and arms of women, children, and the elderly.[22] William Shawcross, who had come to Sierra Leone for the International Crisis Group, has described his visit to Bo, the district capital, where those able to escape arrived with massive injuries. The only surgeon in the town, from Médecins sans Frontières (MSF), carried out thirty operations in one week on people who had double amputations, severed arms, or faces slashed with machete blows. Shawcross was struck by the silence in the wards as people grimly contemplated their future. "The victims were in shock. The thought of their lives ahead was terrible. With one savage blow, or with many awful sawing cuts, they had been deprived of any livelihood, if not of their lives."[23] It was a scene that was to be replayed in the capital city two years later with much greater international publicity.

On the eve of the elections, Attorney General Claude Campbell sought through legal maneuvers to have them put off. Campbell demanded that the electoral rolls that had been reopened to allow for late registration be presented in final form to his office twenty-four hours before the polls opened. This was a technical impossibility, as he well knew. On Sunday, February 25, rumors swept the city that an announcement of cancellation was imminent. The candidates and their supporters were in an uproar. Maada Bio was supposedly unavailable. U.S. deputy chief of mission Charles Ray got hold of NPRC spokesman Karefa Kargbo and obtained agreement for a 9 P.M. meeting. When James Jonah, British high commissioner Ian McCluney, and I met Maada Bio, his deputy Akim Gibril,[24] and Campbell, we listened to a lengthy diatribe about the electoral commission's failure to abide by constitutional procedures and protestations of the NPRC's good intentions. The fact of the meeting, however, was sufficient. Maada Bio had decided he had no choice but to proceed. He was not prepared to shoot down his fellow citizens in the street.

ELECTIONS

On election day, massive crowds turned out in Freetown and the other major cities. People waited patiently in voting lines under the hot sun for hours. When shooting erupted at the Wilberforce Barracks in the late afternoon, voters stood their ground. On Siaka Stevens Street in the heart of downtown Freetown, soldiers trying to disrupt the elections faced a defiant public and retreated. Late that afternoon, Maada Bio announced that the elections would be extended for an additional day. When the votes were finally tallied, 750,000 ballots had been cast, but a runoff was required as none of the presidential candidates had received the required 55 percent of the vote.

In the two weeks until the runoff, the RUF—notwithstanding the promise of its representatives in Abidjan to continue negotiations for an end to the fighting—intensified its campaign of attacking villages in the north and indiscriminately amputated arms and legs of innocent villagers. Women and children, old and young men; it made no difference. Hands and arms were hacked off by machetes, sending a message that others would lose their limbs if they used their hands to mark a ballot paper. In makeshift facilities in Bo and Kenema, MSF and ICRC staff provided emergency medical care. Remarkably, these amputations received virtually no international media attention, largely because they took place far away from the capital city. Thousands of frightened people poured into Kambia and Makeni. The RUF's message was clear: similar treatment awaited all those who supported the elections. It was a tactic that the RUF would use repeatedly over the next years. These events were harbingers of the scenes that were to become all too familiar in the international media in 1998–1999.

Notwithstanding the RUF's brutal tactics, the voter turnout reached 1 million, in part because the army—in a late effort to show its support—facilitated the distribution of ballot papers to remote villages. Ahmed Tejan Kabbah, the leader of the Sierra Leone People's Party (SLPP), defeated John Karefa Smart, the leader of the United National People's Party, 59 to

Associated Press AP

Newly elected president of Sierra Leone, Ahmed Tejan Kabbah waves to voters after casting his ballot on March 15, 1996, in the capital Freetown during the country's first presidential election in more than a decade. Sierra Leone had been under military rule since April 1992.

Gary Schulz

Police oversight during the February 26–27, 1996, election in Freetown.

41 percent. Despite a number of irregularities, the international observers pronounced it a free and fair election.[25] Charges of massive voter fraud focused mainly on the SLPP's stronghold in the south, where many more ballots were cast than there were registered voters. Karefa Smart and another presidential candidate, Abass Bundu, in an angry meeting on election night with Commissioner Jonah, demanded a recount and a delay in announcing the results.[26] Jonah referred them to the courts and announced Kabbah's victory at 9 P.M. Despite the curfew, jubilant crowds poured into the streets. On March 29, Brigadier General Maada Bio handed over the mace to President Kabbah, in one of the few instances of a peaceful handover of power from the military to an elected civilian leader, and the promise of peace followed the new president as he rode in an open car around the streets of Freetown. But underneath this idyllic picture the junior officers and others who lost out in the transition were already nursing

their grievances on the outskirts of the city. After the May 1997 coup, Karefa Smart and Bundu proposed establishment of a transitional government instead of restoration of the Kabbah government, fueling suspicions that they sought to exploit the coup and its aftermath to advance their own interests. The legacy of distrust and suspicion between them and the SLPP over the conduct of the 1996 election has never been overcome.

NOTES

1. The NPRC officers appointed competent civil servants as governor of the Central Bank and to other key portfolios. Tight fiscal policies garnered high marks from IMF officials in Washington, and led to extended budgetary support notwithstanding the internal lack of accountability, especially as regarded funds allocated to the army and the war effort.

2. At the time, Hilton Fyle was the most famous African working for the BBC Africa Service. He had a worldwide audience and his opinions were highly regarded. For Sierra Leoneans, he had demonstrated a level of professionalism reached only by two other Sierra Leonean broadcasters of an earlier generation, John Akar and John Bankole-Jones. For Strasser and associates, Fyle's praise was a big achievement as it gave their coup legitimacy.

3. These cases were under review by a specially appointed tribunal headed by Justice Cross, a prominent Trinidadian jurist, before the proceedings were interrupted by the May 1997 coup.

4. Abdul K. Koroma, *Sierra Leone: The Agony of a Nation* (United Kingdom: Andromeda Publications, 1996), p. 213.

5. Among those executed were Inspector General of Police Bambe Kamara, arguably the most powerful and hated man under the Momoh regime, and the first woman ever executed by any government in Sierra Leone. There also are doubts as to whether the executions happened as reported. One version contended that Strasser's deputy, S.A.J. Musa, shot some of the condemned in Pademba Road Prison, and another held that some were hacked to death before being taken for burial in an unmarked grave at Kingtom cemetery.

6. The AFRC-RUF junta recorded these executions on videotape. An edited version was shown to the UN Special Conference on Sierra Leone, July 30, 1998.

7. Just before handing power to Momoh, Stevens sent deputy chief of staff Brigadier Sam King into early retirement. While King had put down several coup attempts, Stevens feared him. His successor, Brigadier Tarawallie, was notoriously corrupt and indifferent to casualties under his command. Interview, Syl Cheney-Coker, August 1999.

8. Barrie subsequently joined Fayia Musa and others in seeking Sankoh's removal from the leadership of the RUF. In late March 1997, he and four others were captured by RUF field commander Sam Bockarie in Kailahun and held in severe conditions until late 1999.

9. See Paul Richards, *Fighting for the Rainforest: War, Youth, and Resources in Sierra Leone* (Oxford: James Currey, 1998) for an in-depth account of the RUF strategy.

10. These events were reported by Victor Sylver on the BBC *Focus on Africa* radio program; text printed as "Rebels Without a Cause," undated.

11. See Elizabeth Rubin, "An Army of One's Own," *Harpers* (February 1997): 44–55.

12. See William Reno, *Warlord Politics and African States* (Boulder, CO: Lynne Rienner Publishers, 1999), pp. 113–146; David Shearer, "Private Armies and Military Intervention," *IISS Adelphi Paper* 316, (Oxford: Oxford University Press, February 1998), pp. 49–53.

13. Reno, *Warlord Politics*, p. 129.

14. Shearer, "Private Armies," p. 42.

15. Branch Energy and Executive Outcomes were reportedly partly owned by Strategic Resources of Pretoria, South Africa; Branch Energy also had ties to Heritage Oil and Gas, which had operated in Angola while EO was providing similar services to the Angolan government. See Reno, *Warlord Politics*, p. 131.

16. Interview with Captain Valentine Strasser en route to the fiftieth anniversary celebration at the United Nations, October 1995.

17. In 1967 Norman played a key role in the first coup attempt against an elected president. Army Commander David Lansana ordered Hinga Norman, then aide-de-camp (ADC) to Governor General Henry Lightfoot Boston, to halt the swearing-in ceremony. As the ceremony had already taken place, Lansana ordered Norman to hold Stevens in custody. Stevens went briefly into exile in Guinea. Interview with Syl Cheney-Coker, October 18, 1999.

18. Shearer, "Private Armies," pp. 50–51.

19. Article 12 of the Abidjan Peace Agreement provided for Executive Outcomes' withdrawal to take place "five weeks after the deployment of the Neutral Monitoring Group," an international structure for "monitoring breaches of the ceasefire" that was never established. See *Peace Agreement Between the Government of the Republic of Sierra Leone and the Revolutionary United Front of Sierra Leone*, signed at Abidjan on November 30, 1996, S/1996/1034.

20. The February 25 and 28 meetings, just before and after the election, were attended on the RUF side by Faya Musa, Dean Jalloh, Mohamed Barrie, and Agnes Jalloh; the NPRC delegation included Tom Nyuma and Charles Mbayo. Interview with Kathryn Jones, UN Department of Political Affairs, February 18, 2000.

21. Confidential interviews.

22. RUF atrocities have precedent in Africa. Belgian policy in the Congo Free State under King Leopold involved cutting off hands, ears, and noses of people in order to maintain the requisite quota of rubber and ivory collection. See Adam Hochschild, *King Leopold's Ghost: A Story of Greed, Terror and Heroism in Colonial Africa* (New York: Houghton Mifflin, 1999), pp. 164–166.

23. See William Shawcross, *Deliver Us From Evil: Peacekeepers, Warlords, and a World of Endless Conflict* (New York: Simon and Schuster, 2000), pp. 200–203.

24. Gibril, a medical doctor by training, played a disgraceful role the same month in delaying medical care for Minister of Lands Paul Kamara, former editor of *For Di People*, who had been beaten up and shot in the leg by government thugs in retaliation for his earlier criticism of the NPRC. To compound the offense, the NPRC then gave the London clinic a check that promptly bounced. Kamara has never fully recovered from his injuries.

25. See African-American Institute, *Sierra Leone: A Final Report* (Washington, D.C.: The African-American Institute, December 1996), as well as Commonwealth, *Report of the Commonwealth Observer Group to the Presidential and Parliamentary Elections in Sierra Leone*, April 1996.

26. In the early 1990s Abbas Bundu had been ECOWAS executive secretary,

where he played a pivotal role in the formation of ECOMOG and its intervention in Liberia. Subsequently, he served briefly as NPRC foreign minister. After Kabbah came into office, he was tried for fraud involving the sale of passports to Hong Kong businessmen. Rather than go to jail, Bundu repaid the government over $100,000 of the $200,000 he had allegedly collected.

3

The Kabbah Presidency
and the Army/RUF Coup

The new government's top priority was finding a way to restore peace to Sierra Leone. Over the eight months from Kabbah's inauguration to the signing of the Abidjan Agreement, there was a close relationship between the on-again, off-again negotiating process in the Côte d'Ivoire and the shifting balance of forces in the fighting in eastern Sierra Leone. The Revolutionary United Front's (RUF) approach to the negotiations was significantly influenced by the increasing success of Executive Outcomes and Kamajoh operations on the ground. It was therefore understandable that among the RUF's top priorities was the withdrawal of foreign forces, while from the government's viewpoint this was a bargaining chip to be held in reserve until issues of power sharing and the amnesty could be resolved.

Kabbah and Sankoh met for the first time in Yamoussoukro on April 23–24, 1996, after which their delegations began detailed negotiations in Abidjan in May. The Freetown government team was led by Attorney General Solomon Berewa and Desmond Luke, a prominent attorney who had served as Sierra Leone's foreign minister under Stevens. The RUF team was led by Fayia Musa and Ibrahim Dean Jalloh, both of whom had been teachers before they were kidnapped by the RUF in the early 1990s and joined the rebels. It was perhaps inevitable that the two sides were deeply skeptical of each other's motives. According to one observer, the RUF viewed the government side as too legalistic, while the government believed the RUF was using the talks only to buy time. Sankoh reportedly had been advised that discontent within the army would soon lead to a coup and therefore there was no need for the RUF to make concessions. At the same time it was probably the case that the RUF team, having emerged from the bush after five years of guerrilla fighting, was uncertain as to how it would be received by the Sierra Leonean public.[1]

Most problematic was the role of International Alert, a London-based nongovernmental organization (NGO), as the RUF's foreign policy strategist. Kumar Rupesinghe, International Alert's secretary-general at the time, and his colleague Akyaaba Sebo, a free-lance Ghanaian journalist, had their own agenda for the talks: to earn international acclaim for resolving the conflict. At the same time, they worked to change the public perception of the RUF from ruthless rebels to legitimate representatives of the oppressed. They encouraged the RUF to take maximal positions.[2] Organization for African Unity (OAU) representative Adowa Coleman also advised the RUF, and her role seemed to a number of observers as partisan. United Nations Special Envoy Berhanu Dinka, having resided for over a year in Freetown and with daily contact with the government, was viewed by the RUF with suspicion. Sankoh later was to bitterly attack Dinka as biased; Sankoh regarded the entire UN system as being against him. The Commonwealth representative, Moses Anafu, while residing in London, faced some of the same criticism as Dinka.

Nonetheless the Abidjan negotiations proceeded with Ivorian foreign minister Amara Essy working diligently to keep the two sides engaged. After reaching agreement on twenty-six of twenty-eight points, talks broke off in late May over the RUF demand for the withdrawal of all foreign forces—that is, Executive Outcomes and the Nigerian army Training Team—as a precondition for their signing the agreement. Withdrawal of these groups would have left the government forces extremely vulnerable should the RUF renege on the agreement; the condition was rejected by the government. Sankoh also kept pressing his demand for the vice presidency and privately complained to Essy that it had been promised him by Maada Bio. Essy believed Kabbah should find a way to accommodate Sankoh even if this meant amending or bypassing the 1991 Constitution. Kabbah, however, insisted that the constitution would not allow the vice presidency to go to someone who had not even taken part in the election and that the parliament would impeach him if he tried to push through Sankoh's appointment. Underneath the constitutional argument was concern that Sankoh would use his appointment to a senior position in Freetown as a launching pad for taking power through a palace coup. Many of the same issues would arise two years later, but in a radically changed political context. Interestingly, the least controversial issue was the granting of amnesty, even though the RUF had committed extensive atrocities in the run-up to the election.[3]

KAMAJOHS

In the meantime, the war in southern and eastern Sierra Leone had taken a new turn that was ultimately to have a decisive bearing on the talks. Traditional hunters, known as Kamajohs, emerged as a new military force. Coming from a long tradition of self-defense of rural villages, these forces had different names in different sections of the country (Tamaboros in the north). When Chief Hinga Norman, who had been a prominent leader of the Kamajohs as well as a retired military officer, was appointed as the new deputy defense minister, he had little confidence in the army. Upon assuming office, he turned his energies to mobilizing the Kamajohs to help defeat the RUF. Previously, these civil-defense forces had largely limited themselves to defending major towns; they now undertook at his direction to engage in hot pursuit of the RUF in the bush.

Norman was highly regarded by the Mende power brokers, perhaps because of the role he played in the 1967 coup seeking to block Stevens from assuming office. They viewed him as well-suited to protect their interests in maintaining Mende political control. As Kabbah's senior military adviser, Norman promptly took the highly controversial stand of distancing himself from the army. Convinced that the military were acting in collusion with the RUF, and aware of their dismal role in repelling the rebels, Norman threw his support behind the Kamajohs. In practical terms, Norman had few resources to offer the Kamajohs, but he used them as personal bodyguards when he moved around the country, thus building up their prestige to the considerable anger and frustration of the army leadership. (Interestingly, Norman and Sankoh had been in prison together in 1971 for their roles in a failed coup attempt against Siaka Stevens. Norman was released, whereas Sankoh remained in jail for a number of years. Norman probably understood Sankoh's mentality and frustrations better than anyone else in the cabinet.)

The Kamajohs battled on two fronts—against both the RUF and the army. By early autumn the combination of Executive Outcomes and Kamajoh operations had put the RUF under severe pressure.[4] The Kamajohs had a "take no prisoners" policy and it was widely assumed that there were significant RUF casualties. This could never be corroborated, as both the Kamajohs and the rebels quickly buried their dead. UK military adviser Colonel Andrew Gayle believed that by mid-October the RUF was on the threshold of being decisively defeated, and that this was the main motive for Sankoh's decision to sign the Abidjan Agreement.[5] In early November, Sankoh indicated he was ready to drop the RUF's demand for prior withdrawal of foreign forces. He insisted, however, that he had to consult with his field commanders on the terms of the agreement that was to put a formal end to the five-and-a-half-year-old conflict. After considerable procrastination, ostensibly out of security concerns, Sankoh was taken in mid-November by an International Committee of the Red Cross (ICRC) helicopter to meet with his field commanders in the Kangari Hills, Bradford and Kailahun.

The Abidjan Agreement's signing ceremony took place on Saturday, November 30.[6] The Ivorians sent a special airplane to take President Kabbah and his forty-person delegation to Abidjan. The aircraft arrived

late, and the signing, which was to take place at noon, got under way at
4 P.M. In addition to the two principal signatories, there were four moral
guarantors who signed the accord—the UN, the Commonwealth, the OAU,
and the Côte d'Ivoire government.[7] Radio transmission of the ceremony to
Freetown broke off halfway through the ceremony. A brief reception followed the signing. President Kabbah and his associates departed shortly
afterwards in order to get back to Freetown in time for a large nighttime
celebration. Kabbah turned down the proposal that Ivorian president Bedie,
Sankoh, and he return together to Freetown. That Sankoh was regarded as
too unpopular to be seen in Freetown was itself a sign of how much suspicion remained. Sierra Leoneans, however, were enthusiastic about the
agreement and later greeted Musa and Jalloh with adulation when they
traveled in early 1997 to Bo and Kenema.

COLLAPSE OF THE ABIDJAN PEACE AGREEMENT

No sooner was the Abidjan Agreement signed than the nascent peace
process began to break down. On the surface, preliminary steps at implementation were taking place. Sankoh and Kabbah were in almost daily telephone contact. Arrangements were made for four RUF members (Fayia
Musa, Ibrahim Deen Jalloh, Agnes Deen Jalloh, and Michael Sandy) to
come to Freetown for the formal December 19 launch of the Commission
for the Consolidation of Peace (CCP), whose role was to oversee implementation of the peace agreement.

The peace accord had established the CCP with eight members (four
government, four RUF).[8] The RUF officials who had come to Freetown
received a warm reception and over the next two months gradually came to
see the benefits of the peace agreement. They became convinced that the
Abidjan Agreement was genuinely popular and reconciliation attainable. In
the meantime, Sankoh was delaying the appointment of RUF members to
the Disarmament and Demobilization Committee, which was to designate
the locations for demobilization.

In mid-December Sankoh complained to Essy that the Freetown government was not honoring the cease-fire. He charged that the Kamajohs
were still attacking RUF positions. The Sierra Leone army, in turn, inter-
cepted a radio message from Sankoh to his field commanders saying that he
signed the accord only to relieve the military pressure and that he intended
to purchase new arms and continue the war.[9] Kabbah confronted Sankoh on
the telephone (they were holding lengthy daily phone conversations); angry
words were exchanged. By mid-January 1997 communication between the
two leaders collapsed. Instead of trying to reestablish contact, Kabbah sent
his foreign minister, Shirley Gbujama, to explain Sierra Leone's position to
the leaders in the region.

At about the same time, Jalloh and Musa concluded that Sankoh had no intention of honoring the accords. The CCP members traveled to Abidjan in late February. Sankoh declined to see them as a delegation but invited each one to come separately to his house. Sensing a trap, they refused. No contact took place.

Early in the morning of March 6, Sankoh traveled covertly to Lagos with two associates purportedly on a personal visit that the government later suspected was an arms-purchasing mission. On leaving Mohammed Murtala Airport, he was stopped in the parking lot by Nigerian police. They discovered rounds of ammunition in the car and arrested him. Twelve hours later the Nigerians took Sankoh to Abuja after figuring out that he was the RUF leader and not just an ordinary criminal. Nigerian head of state Sani Abacha reportedly phoned Kabbah, who asked that Sankoh be kept in protective custody.[10] For several months Sankoh lived at the Sheraton Hotel in Abuja. When he succeeded in communicating with his field commanders, including through BBC interviews, the Nigerians moved him to a safe house elsewhere in Abuja where he was held virtually incommunicado for eighteen months, including the entire period of Armed Forces Revolutionary Council (AFRC)/RUF junta control in Freetown. In July 1998, by agreement between Nigerian head of state General Abubakr and Kabbah (who had returned from his own forced exile in Guinea four months earlier), Sankoh was returned to Freetown to stand trial for treason.[11]

THE INTERNAL RUF COUP FAILS

After their rebuff by Sankoh, Musa and Deen Jalloh became convinced that a change of RUF leadership was necessary if the peace accord was to be implemented. They recognized that they would need the support of key field commanders in order to win the support of the rank and file, many of whom were still fighting in the bush. They established radio contact with Philip Palmer, one of the RUF's senior military commanders. On March 16, 1997, speaking from the village of Danane on the Ivorian/Liberian border, Palmer announced that Sankoh was no longer the leader of the RUF in view of his refusal to implement the Abidjan Agreement; he indicated that a new leadership for the RUF would be announced shortly thereafter.[12]

Musa and Deen Jalloh traveled to Conakry, where they were joined by Sierra Leone's ambassador to Guinea, Colonel Diaby, who was designated as the government's representative on the delegation. They proceeded to Guekedou in eastern Guinea, separated from Kailahun in eastern Sierra Leone by the Mano River. A political conclave of senior RUF commanders was to take place on Guinean territory to announce the appointment of Sankoh's successor. Sam Bockarie, Sankoh's second in command, invited the RUF Freetown delegation to cross the river to Kailahun for a big feast to be followed by agreement on the new leadership. Despite being warned that this was a trap, Musa, Deen Jalloh, Palmer, and Sankoh's physician Dr. Mohamed Barrie, as well as Diaby, crossed over from Guinea and were immediately seized and incarcerated. Several Guinean soldiers who accompanied them managed to avoid capture, and at least one of the soldiers drowned in the river while trying to return to the Guinean side. Bockarie immediately charged them with treason for denouncing Sankoh's leadership of the movement and seeking to appoint another leader.[13] Diaby's release three months later and his return to Conakry fueled suspicion that he was a double agent. For over two years, efforts first by Kabbah and Desmond Luke, and then by their families, to find out whether the four captured men were alive or dead, and to obtain medical access to them, went unheeded. Musa and Deen Jalloh were released in November 1999 after two and a half years of incarceration, during which they were probably tortured. The fate of the others is still unclear.

AFRC/RUF JUNTA INTERREGNUM

The May 25, 1997, coup was organized by junior army officers based at Goderich, just west of Freetown. Two previous coup attempts had been thwarted. One junior officer arrested in the first coup attempt in September 1996 was Major Johnny Paul Koroma, a Sandhurst graduate. Junior officers had lost their prestige and perquisites in the transition from the military regime to a civilian government. Despite Kabbah's assurances to the army that there would not be any precipitous downsizing, there were rumors of imminent demobilization without the provision of pensions or any preparation for returning to civilian life. As a number of these officers had been close to Strasser and Maada Bio, they were well aware that the National Provisional Ruling Council's youthful leaders had looted the nation's assets, purchased properties abroad, and obtained UN-funded scholarships in England and the United States in exchange for relinquishing power. Significantly, ethnic and regional politics also played a role. All the coup plotters came from one Limba chiefdom in the north, the home of former president Momoh. They were deeply suspicious not only of Kabbah but also of what they perceived as Sierra Leone People's Party (SLPP) ambitions to maintain indefinite political dominance. Their spokesman, Corporal Tamba Gborie, in announcing the coup, claimed the officers were opposed to the government's acts of "tribalism" and corruption and its suspension of freedom of the press. "The people had fought for democracy but never got it."[14]

The army's upper ranks were also rife with resentment at Kabbah's tacit support for Chief Norman and the Kamajohs. In the lower ranks, there was considerable bitterness about low salaries (when they were paid at all) and the reduction in the rice ration. At the IMF's insistence to bring down military expenditures, Kabbah had cut the rice ration from 40,000 to 34,000 bags a month. This should have been enough to feed the army even at the inflated roll of 17,000 troops (there were probably 10,000–12,000 troops at the time). The top echelons of the army, however, were siphoning off rice for their own use and reselling it commercially.[15] Moreover, Chief of Defense Staff Hassan Conteh and Chief of Army Staff Max Kanga were misrepresenting the security situation to President Kabbah. On May 6 the RUF (which supposedly was on its last legs) broke out of its encirclement at Bradford and marched unimpeded 100 miles to the north to capture the border town of Kamikwe. Then they wheeled back, advancing on Makeni and Port Loko. The speed of the rebel movements pointed to collusion with the army. When Conteh tried to order troops at the Benguema training center east of Freetown to engage the RUF in the north, a third of them refused to go, took off their uniforms, and deserted.[16] Conteh and Kanga didn't bother to report these developments to the president. The stage for the coup was set.

SPRINGING THE TRAP

On Sunday, May 25, at 3 A.M., while most people slept peacefully, the army plotters broke open the arsenal at Murray Town barracks. Shortly thereafter gunshots erupted. Troops with red shirts began roaming the city. Around 6 A.M. they blew open the front door of Pademba Road Prison. The soldiers freed all the prisoners, including Major Johnny Paul Koroma, who was promptly declared chairman of the AFRC. Suddenly thousands of soldiers wearing red shirts and bandanas were roaming the city, looting, raping, and shooting at random. Marine Corporal Joe Arnold and his Sierra Leonean driver, en route to the U.S. Embassy for a duty shift, had their vehicle commandeered at gunpoint. Arnold was forced to take the soldiers to the Aqua Club, a small marina where a number of private boats were anchored, before being released. When he arrived at the embassy, near State House, the siege was under way in full force. Before the day was over, the area around State House was a scene of devastation. Over the next few days the Nigerian Embassy and United Nations Headquarters were trashed. The adjacent U.S. Embassy lost ninety-six windows to gunfire but remained virtually intact and was never penetrated. Over the next several weeks gangs roamed the city at will, looting houses and killing civilians arbitrarily. The World Food Program warehouse and other storehouses were also looted. In the meantime, reinforced Nigerian units took control of the airport. This started the seesaw battle for control of the city over the next nine months, bringing to an end the buoyant first phase of Sierra Leone's democratic venture.

There were an estimated four hundred UN and diplomatic personnel in

Freetown at the time (as well as several thousand Lebanese and other foreign residents). As the coup took place early on a Sunday morning, virtually all UN and diplomatic personnel were either in their residences or at one or another of the small beach hotels on the Freetown peninsula. While volleys of rocket-launched grenades fell around State House, the rebelling soldiers quickly took over the television and radio stations. Confusion and panic gripped the city. U.S. charge d'affaires Ann Wright took the lead in establishing communications between British high commissioner Penfold, Nigerian high commissioner Abubakr, and UN Special Envoy Dinka even as they were pinned down in their residences. Wright informed the State Department, which went into a crisis mode, establishing a task force in its seventh-floor operations center. The British and French governments also were informed, and focused their attention on organizing aircraft and maritime rescue of their citizens. The government ministers hunkered down in their residences. Chief Norman, at considerable risk to himself, tried in vain to find loyal forces to defend against the rampaging soldiers. Later in the day he hid in the elevator shaft of the Mammy Yoko Hotel in the far west of the city, where he stayed for five days until he could be rescued as part of the U.S. evacuation. President Kabbah, with only his personal security staff by his side, left his residence around 11:30 A.M. He was driven to Kabassa Lodge, on high ground west of the city center (ironically the former residence of Siaka Stevens). Shortly before noon he left by helicopter for the thirty-minute flight into exile in Conakry.

NEGOTIATIONS AND RESCUE

The efforts of the international community over the next week can be divided into two parts: (1) trying to persuade the army coup leaders to step down and allow President Kabbah to resume office, and (2) arranging for the evacuation of over three thousand foreigners. Diplomats, humanitarian aid workers, missionaries, and long-term residents (mainly West African and Lebanese nationals, including a large number of women and children) left Freetown. At a meeting late on May 30 at the residence of the British high commissioner, the four diplomats sought to persuade the junta to abandon their efforts and leave peacefully with appropriate guarantees. Interestingly, the negotiating points under consideration in their discussion with Koroma that night contained many of the elements of the Lomé Peace Agreement signed just over two years later.[17] The initial signs of willingness to consider an amnesty and accept safe passage to Nigeria ended, however, as soon as the RUF joined the army officers in Freetown. The RUF, which had waited for six years for this moment, took command. From then on junta chairman Johnny Paul Koroma could not have left Freetown even if he had wanted to, as the more radical RUF leaders would surely have killed him.

While the residents of Freetown were being brutalized by marauding gangs, the evacuation of foreigners proceeded in an atmosphere of great anxiety and trepidation. Several foreigners were raped and a few were killed. Koroma later apologized and there were reports that the alleged perpetrators were summarily executed. Freetown's topography made the departure of international staff and families, as well as foreign nationals, extraordinarily difficult to organize. With Lungi International Airport located across the broad estuary of the harbor, the only two helicopters being operated commercially in the country ferried over five hundred people from a helipad next to the Mammy Yoko Hotel to hastily organized British and Belgian charter flights. A French frigate came from Conakry to remove several hundred foreigners and a small number of Sierra Leoneans from a makeshift dock on the Aberdeen peninsula. In Washington, D.C., the Pentagon ordered the *USS Kearsarge*, stationed fortuitously off the coast of Congo a thousand miles to the south (where it had been preparing for a possible evacuation of U.S. citizens from Zaire), to steam toward Freetown. The *Kearsarge* arrived late on May 29. The next day, Charge Wright mobilized the embassy staff to coordinate the evacuation of eight hundred foreigners, including a large number of women and children, by helicopters to the multipurpose amphibious assault ship anchored ten miles offshore. The *Kearsarge*, after taking the evacuees to Conakry, returned unexpectedly to Freetown twice in the next two days. On May 31, the ship picked up a group of orphans and other Americans who had not shown up for the first day of evacuations. Then, most dramatically, the *Kearsarge* returned once again on June 1–2 for a rescue from Lumley Beach of over twelve hundred U.S. and third-country nationals in the largest single-day evacuation in navy and marine history.

On the morning of June 1, the Nigerians shelled the port area from a gunboat in the harbor, believing that this would force the junta to flee. Instead, they precipitated a massive RUF attack on the small contingent of Nigerian forces guarding the perimeter of the Mammy Yoko Hotel, where over eight hundred foreigners had taken shelter. The RUF attack overwhelmed the Nigerian ECOMOG forces, who ran out of ammunition after ten hours of heavy fighting. Using rocket-propelled grenades and an antiaircraft gun, the RUF set the hotel on fire, and the civilians trapped inside retreated to the basement. Around 4 P.M., with the intervention of ICRC representative Laurent Fellay, a fragile cease-fire was negotiated. Close to sunset, the terrified and exhausted crowd left the hotel. Most went to the adjacent Cape Sierra Hotel to await helicopter rescue by the *Kearsarge* the next morning. Others returned to the city under the ICRC flag. Over the coming days and weeks, scores and then hundreds of Sierra Leoneans would struggle to find their way to Conakry and Banjul by boats or vehicles.

President Kabbah and an estimated two hundred thousand Sierra Leoneans went into exile. The fortunate few who reached Conakry or Banjul, and had families and friends in Europe and the United States, were able to leave the region. Those without financial means or family connections became refugees in Guinea, joining those who had fled over the previous six years to live in the refugee camps in the border areas at Fourekaria and Guekedou. The cycle of violence and displacement continued mercilessly.

REGIONAL PEACEKEEPING:
THE OAU AND THE EVOLVING ROLE OF ECOWAS

For President Kabbah and his close associates these were bitter months. Uncertainty and confusion were somewhat attenuated by the strong political support they received from the OAU and the Economic Community of West African States (ECOWAS). The junta takeover came on the eve of the annual OAU heads-of-state summit meeting in Harare, Zimbabwe. UN Secretary-General Kofi Annan called on the assembled leaders to condemn the coup, stating that

> Africa can no longer tolerate and accept as *faits accomplis,* coups against elected governments, and the illegal seizure of power by military cliques, who sometimes act for sectional interests, sometimes simply for their own. Armies exist to protect national sovereignty, not to train their guns on their own people . . . Verbal condemnation, though necessary and desirable, is not sufficient. We must also ostracize and isolate putschists. Neighboring States, regional groupings, and the international community all must play their part.[18]

James Jonah, who had become Sierra Leone's permanent representative to the United Nations, flew directly from New York to appeal for action to restore the elected government. It was a unique moment in African politics and a striking departure from the traditional OAU stance of noninterference in the internal affairs of member states. Among the heads of state present in the chamber were many who themselves had come to power through military coups.[19] The OAU asked ECOWAS, whose military arm was deeply engaged at the moment in assuring security for Liberia's upcoming presidential elections, to consider how best to bring about Kabbah's restoration. ECOWAS was asked to take all necessary measures to persuade the junta to step down. The heads of state were doubtlessly aware that another successful coup by junior officers could set a dangerous precedent for their own regimes. That said, the OAU was considerably less forceful in responding to the coup in Congo Brazzaville the next month.

In the first week after the coup, many Sierra Leoneans thought the takeover would be short-lived. After the June 1 fiasco, however, it was clear that the Nigerian military had misjudged the situation. The local commander whose troops had been stranded at the Mammy Yoko Hotel without adequate communication, logistics, ammunition, or backup was quickly recalled to Abuja. The Nigerians lacked sufficient forces on the ground and were in no position to launch a full-fledged assault against the junta in the complex Freetown setting. Nine hundred additional troops were quickly flown in to Lungi and Hastings to supplement the seven hundred troops already based there.

The issue of how to deal with the coup brought to the surface deep-rooted divisions within ECOWAS, particularly the underlying ambivalence of Ghana and Côte d'Ivoire about Nigeria's dominant political and military position in the subregion. Nigeria, with a population of over 100 million people and a standing army and air force of 71,500 men, inevitably had the greatest capacity to project a regional security presence. Ghana, a country of 18 million, had its own well-trained army but of much smaller dimension.[20] Some tensions were already present in Liberia, where the two countries were the core of the ECOMOG forces. Côte d'Ivoire, in contrast, saw itself as a political rather than military force in the subregion, and had taken the primary role in the negotiations leading to the Abidjan Agreement. In the summer of 1997, Bedie and Essy reluctantly ceded that role to Abacha and Ikimi. There was also the question of Nigeria's relations with National Patriotic Front of Liberia leader Charles Taylor. Abacha in the early 1990s had supported Taylor, but the two men had fallen out when it became clear that Taylor had his own aspirations for regional leadership.

In Sierra Leone, the Nigerians clearly favored a military solution, but the inability to attain a decisive combat victory at the outset forced them to change their strategy. Ghana and Côte d'Ivoire urged negotiations. They were not convinced that the situation could be reversed by force. Moreover, as Ghana's foreign minister Victor Gbeho put it, ECOWAS should not require Africans to kill each other if some other solution can be found. At a meeting in Conakry at the end of June, the ECOWAS foreign ministers decided to pursue three tracks sequentially—dialogue, sanctions, and, only if necessary, the use of force.[21] They formed a Committee of Four (C-4)—Nigeria, Côte d'Ivoire, Ghana, and Guinea—that was instructed to open up contact with the junta leaders. The prospect of a protracted dialogue added to the frustration and sense of impotence among Kabbah's inner circle. While the president remained confident that ECOWAS would prevail and accepted its decisions with apparent equanimity, his advisers, especially James Jonah and Desmond Luke, as well as British high commissioner Penfold, were pressing him to seek a more aggressive stance from Abacha.

THE REGIONAL SEARCH FOR A DIPLOMATIC SOLUTION

The AFRC/RUF junta was determined to derive maximum political and financial advantage from its control of Freetown. They wanted at one and the same time to obtain legitimacy for their action, claiming as their justification Kabbah's failure to carry out his commitments under the Abidjan Agreement, and to retain their control of Freetown for as long as possible. They also wanted to deny President Kabbah and his elected government the right to return while claiming to have acted in accordance with the 1991 Constitution. The junta's strategy, which emerged over the next two months, was to buy time without suffering international opprobrium by offering various proposals for the restoration of constitutional government through power sharing, establishment of a transitional government, or early elections. At the same time, as a condition for their cooperation, the junta pressed for the release of Foday Sankoh, appointed vice chairman of the AFRC in absentia, from his continued detention in Nigeria.

The Freetown junta was directly or indirectly supported in these objectives by a number of anti-SLPP politicians. Former president Momoh (who had been allowed by Kabbah to return to Freetown several months earlier) became a formal adviser to the junta. John Karefa Smart and Abass Bundu, who had contested the 1996 election and were now resident in London, offered to serve as mediators. Each saw the coup as an opportunity to redress grievances and abort the contested results of the 1996 election.[22]

Throughout this period, not a single government or multilateral organization recognized the AFRC/RUF junta or accepted its rationale for the coup. In Freetown, popular resistance continued as many shops remained closed and trade unions, schoolteachers, and newspaper editors refused to cooperate. Regime efforts to organize staged demonstrations of support failed. While the junta's international public-relations campaign fizzled, in the short term its ability to maintain external lines for petroleum and small arms through the Freetown peninsula and the interior was more important. Weapons, ammunition, and other supplies were reportedly being shipped from Monrovia to small fishing villages on the Freetown peninsula. There were also reports of arms shipments by chartered airplanes from the Ukraine through Burkina Faso to a reconstructed landing strip near Magburaka.[23]

Of even greater political and psychological importance for the Freetown junta, Charles Taylor was elected president of Liberia on July 19 and was inaugurated on August 2, 1997. It was the culmination of a decade-long internal and regional struggle in which Taylor had overcome his rivals, and then positioned himself as the only leader who could bring durable peace to Liberia. Even though Sankoh was still under detention in Abuja, Taylor's legitimization could not have been lost on those who had seized power in Freetown.

Nonetheless, ECOWAS persevered in its efforts to find a diplomatic solution to bring about Kabbah's restoration to office in Freetown. Discussions in Abidjan on July 18–19 between the Committee of Four and the junta's "foreign minister," Pallo Bangura, were abruptly cut off when Johnny Paul Koroma announced defiantly on Sierra Leone Broadcasting System (SLBS) radio that he intended to stay in office until 2001.[24]

At the ECOWAS heads-of-state summit in Abuja (August 26–28), President Kabbah characterized the junta takeover as ushering in "a long night of barbarism and darkness" and gave a vigorous rebuttal of junta charges that he had failed the nation. His "preferred order for the settlement of the present problem in Sierra Leone" was "the immediate and unconditional restoration of . . . [his] government" as demanded by ECOWAS, the OAU, and the UN; the establishment of a "solid security system"; and complete disarmament and resumption of the implementation of the Abidjan Agreement. Acknowledging the three-tier ECOWAS strategy adopted in Conakry, Kabbah indicated that the decision to embark on the third stage, the use of force, was a matter for ECOWAS to decide.[25] As the president already knew from his private discussions with Abacha and others, that moment had not yet come. The ECOWAS heads of state adopted regional sanctions prohibiting the importation of arms, ammunition, and petroleum products into Sierra Leone and imposing travel restrictions on the junta leaders and their families.[26] The summit also provided the first public occasion outside of Liberia for President Taylor to assert a new role in the subregion. Basking in the glow of his election and new status as a democratically elected president, Taylor pressed for enlargement of the C-4 to include Liberia and called for reinvigoration of the virtually defunct Mano River Union (Liberia, Sierra Leone, and Guinea). It was an indirect challenge to Abacha. While gaining entry to what became the C-5, Taylor found little support for his Mano River Union proposal.

THE INTERNATIONAL ROLE: LITTLE AND LATE

Apart from the actions of the OAU and ECOWAS, the international community was slow to mobilize and reluctant to provide resources in support of President Kabbah's restoration. There were several factors to account for the lukewarm international response. Sierra Leone unfortunately was perceived from outside the African continent as a small, strategically insignificant country. While Western headlines were focused on the war in Bosnia, Sierra Leone's coup received relatively little attention in either the electronic or print media. Moreover, the coup came three years after the major failures and retreats of United Nations forces in Somalia and Rwanda. The U.S. decision enshrined in Presidential Decision Directive (PDD) 25 to virtually withdraw from United Nations peacekeeping operations had dissipated what little political will there was for U.S. engagement in Africa.[27] The sole exception in West Africa was Liberia, where the United States had found the mechanism to provide limited but important financial and logistical support for ECOMOG operations. This included a contractual arrangement with Pacific Architects and Engineers, based in Portland, Oregon, to provide maintenance support for helicopter and vehicle operations. The

State Department's Africa Bureau also persuaded Sweden, the Netherlands, and a few other countries to provide balance-of-payments support to assist Liberia's interim government.

Sierra Leone was perceived in Washington (and Brussels) as essentially a British interest, and it was left to the Tony Blair government to take the lead in mustering international support. The United Kingdom assisted President Kabbah in garnering the minimal essential means to maintain his government in exile in Conakry. Prime Minister Blair invited Kabbah to speak to the Commonwealth Conference in Edinburgh in mid-October, and arranged a series of meetings with potential donors in London as well. That said, the British were resolutely opposed to providing financial or material support to ECOMOG as long as Sani Abacha remained ECOWAS chairman. At the November 1995 Commonwealth Conference in New Zealand, the British had played a key role in passing a strong condemnation of Abacha's harsh human rights record at home and in Nigeria's suspension from the Commonwealth itself.[28] British-Nigerian relations were at a low ebb. Whereas the United States was prepared to separate its bilateral and regional policies, London insisted on a total ban on assistance to Nigeria. As a result, Sierra Leone's plight was understood with sympathy but, with Nigeria as the regional lead, little material support. The Security Council meeting on July 11 issued a presidential statement notable for its vagueness and noncommittal stance: "The Security Council will be ready to take appropriate measures with the objective of restoring the democratically elected government of President Kabbah."[29] It was only after ECOWAS's adoption of regional sanctions that the UN Security Council, three months later, acted to invoke parallel international sanctions (UNSC Resolution 1132).[30] The UN initiative had come from the United Kingdom, a fact that was to haunt the Foreign Office when the Sandline arms scandal erupted in the British press five months later.

FROM THE CONAKRY
AGREEMENT TO KABBAH'S RETURN

During these months, ECOMOG began to incrementally build up a significant military presence based at Lungi and Hastings on the eastern side of the city. Surrounded by ECOMOG forces and feeling the squeeze from the petroleum ban, the Freetown junta agreed to send a delegation to Conakry to discuss a negotiated outcome. On October 23, after an all-night negotiation (with the participation of UN Assistant Secretary-General Ibrahima Fall, ECOWAS executive secretary Kouyate, and ECOWAS's Nigerian Force Commander General Malu), the ECOWAS Committee of Five, led by Nigerian foreign minister Ikimi, and the AFRC/RUF delegation led by Bangura and Eldred Collins, signed the Conakry Accords.[31] The accords provided for a process of disarmament and demobilization of AFRC and RUF elements to begin before the end of 1997. Kabbah's constitutionally elected government was to return to Freetown by April 22, 1998 (six months later). The exiled government, through Attorney General Berewa, was present as an observer but was neither allowed to take part in the negotiations nor to present Kabbah's views. The ECOWAS team, while acting on Kabbah's behalf, recognized that had President Kabbah been consulted, there would have been no agreement that day. While Kabbah subsequently accepted the agreement, many of his advisers were strongly opposed to giving the junta a six-month grace period and continued to argue for the immediate use of force. Their misgivings were understandable given the violence and destruction being inflicted on the Freetown population and in villages throughout the country.

The Freetown junta tried to use the accords as the basis for de facto recognition by the international community and continued to purchase arms and ammunition on the international arms market. They also sought to modify the terms of the agreement by insisting again on the immediate release of Foday Sankoh as well as the reduction of Nigeria's role in ECOMOG before the disarmament process could get under way. When UN Envoy Francis Okelo (who had just arrived on the scene), Kouyate and Malu visited Freetown on November 27, the junta staged a show of public support for their demands. Privately, however, Johnny Paul Koroma indicated he was not at all eager for Sankoh to be released.

Over the next two months as the AFRC/RUF junta continued to bring in arms and ammunition over the border from Liberia and delayed the start of its disarmament, ECOMOG geared up for battle. When ECOMOG troops were attacked in various skirmishes around Freetown and Lungi, the force commander, Colonel Maxwell Khobe, ordered the offensive against the AFRC to begin. Over the week of February 8–14 the second battle of Freetown raged as ECOMOG forces advanced from Hastings/Jui on the eastern outskirts of the city, moving westward toward the city's center. After several days of heavy fighting, the AFRC/RUF forces abandoned Freetown but not before destroying 160 houses, indiscriminately killing civilians, and massively looting as they retreated.[32] Many of the soldiers and rebels withdrew through the western-area peninsula, abandoning a large number of vehicles at the fishing village of Tombo. It remains a mystery why ECOMOG forces were so singularly unsuccessful at preventing their flight. There was some speculation that Koroma paid off Nigerian forces to let them escape.

THE ROLE OF SANDLINE INTERNATIONAL

The role of private security groups in Sierra Leone had changed little since the entry of large diamond-mining corporations sixty years earlier.

As noted in Chapter 1, as early as 1936 the state had relinquished the oversight of security in the diamond fields to companies willing to field their own armies to protect their interests.[33] Thus, with the departure of Executive Outcomes in early 1997, Diamond Works and its subsidiary Branch Energy, holding significant properties in Koindu and elsewhere, were left to maintain their own security.[34] Lifeguard Securities, in effect an Executive Outcomes subsidiary, protected Branch Energy's kimberlite holdings as well as maintaining contracts with Sierra Rutile, several UN relief operations, and international NGOs such as World Vision. Lifeguard was not alone. Other companies sought security roles and subsequent potential access to diamond profits, including British companies Defence Systems Ltd., Sky Air, and Occidental, and U.S. groups Military Professional Resources Inc. (MPRI) and International Charters Inc. (ICI).

Sandline International, established by Colonel Tim Spicer, formerly of the British army, entered the scene following the May coup, reportedly due to its connections to Branch Energy. Sandline sought to assist the Kabbah government in creating a military force to repel the AFRC/RUF junta from Freetown and the Kono diamond fields.

Kabbah first made contact with Sandline shortly after the ECOWAS summit of August 29 sanctioned an ECOMOG intervention. Recognizing that the West African forces were constrained by lack of an explicit UN mandate and a crucial lack of resources for logistics and armaments, Kabbah reportedly negotiated an arrangement with Sandline based on pledges from Rakesh Saxena, a banker wanted for embezzlement in Thailand.[35] Saxena promised payment to Sandline in exchange for certain economic concessions from the government of Sierra Leone.[36] Saxena was going to finance the military operation in two installments: $1.5 million for personnel and start-up costs and, later, $3.5 million for provision and shipment of military support equipment. In late 1997, Tim Spicer, Sandline director, met with Kabbah and ECOMOG officials in Conakry and proposed contingency plans for possible military operations, including support for both the Civil Defense Force (CDF) and ECOMOG. Training of the Kamajohs and resupply of weapons were also mentioned.[37]

By December, Kabbah reportedly had coordinated with the Nigerians in obtaining Sandline's assistance for enhancing their command, control, and communications facilities. By the end of January 1998, Phase I of the Sandline plan had been carried out by the CDF as they effectively isolated RUF/AFRC forces in Bo and Kenema through control of the inner road network.[38] However, Phase II was held up by a delay in shipment of arms when Saxena was arrested in Canada for traveling under a false passport.

Sandline continued to provide transport to senior ECOMOG commanders and even rescued Brigadier Khobe and senior UN officials from an RUF firefight.[39] On February 22, Sandline, through associated Sky Air, flew thirty tons of Bulgarian AK-47 rifles to Sierra Leone, where they were stopped by ECOMOG and consigned at Lungi.[40]

After Kabbah's return to Freetown on March 10, an intense controversy erupted in Great Britain over the role of the Foreign Office in the shipment of Sandline arms. Parliamentary and press reports alleged that the British Foreign Office had known of Sandline's intention to break the UN sanctions. In Parliament, Lord Avebury (a board member of International Alert) asserted that Sandline had carried out its activities with the approval of the Foreign Office in violation of the arms embargo adopted under Security Council Resolution 1132. Sandline's chief executive, Tim Spicer, faced an investigation by British Customs and Excise as to whether the arms shipments constituted a criminal offense under British law. Spicer claimed that he had briefed British officials, including High Commissioner Peter Penfold, and members of the Foreign Office before proceeding to provide military equipment and other forms of assistance to the elected government in exile.[41] He also claimed that both UK and U.S. officials had assured him that Kabbah and ECOMOG were exempt from the UN sanctions regime. In some quarters, Avebury's disclosures were perceived as an effort to unseat Foreign Secretary Cook, who was accused of lax management of the Foreign Office.

The final report to the House of Commons exonerated Cook and his deputy, Tony Lloyd, but asserted that Penfold had been insufficiently sensitive to the comprehensive scope of the prohibition on arms transfers as required under Resolution 1132.[42] From a technical standpoint that criticism was perhaps valid, but some observers construed the arms embargo as applying only to the junta, and not to the elected government as it was patently the intent of that resolution to bring about Kabbah's restoration. Kabbah, in an open letter to Prime Minister Blair, asserted that Sandline had actually played no role in his restoration, and that he had not asked for nor received any support from Penfold or any other official of the British government in seeking the assistance of the security group. However, in the face of Sandline's assertions, Kabbah wrote: "My government's view on this is that there is not charge to answer," maintaining that Resolution 1132 was aimed at the coup leaders and not to his legitimate government.[43] The Sandline affair raises a number of important questions for the future: What should a democratically elected government do when, lacking its own army, it comes under siege? Where is the line to be drawn between relying on ineffectual United Nations troops and the option of a more efficient private security force?

NOTES

1. Confidential interview.

2. For an evaluation of International Alert's role in the mediation process, see Gunner Sørbø, Joanna Macrae, and Lennart Wohlgemuth, "NGOs in Conflict: An Evaluation of International Alert," Chr. Michelsen Institute Report Series, No. 6 (CMI, Bergen, Norway, 1997).

3. The Abidjan Agreement, in Article 14, stated that "to consolidate the peace and promote the cause of national reconciliation, the Government of Sierra Leone shall ensure that no official or judicial action is taken against any member of the RUF/SL in respect of anything done by them in pursuit of their objectives as members of that organization up to the time of the signing of this Agreement. In addition, legislative and other measures necessary to guarantee former RUF/SL combatants, exiles and other persons, currently outside the country for reasons related to the armed conflict shall be adopted ensuring the full exercise of their civil and political rights, with a view to their reintegration within a framework of full legality." *Peace Agreement Between the Government of the Republic of Sierra Leone and the Revolutionary United Front of Sierra Leone*, signed at Abidjan on November 30, 1996, S/1996/1034.

4. The reputation of the Kamajohs and Executive Outcomes may have played an important role in pushing back the RUF. Many of the Kamajoh battles were rumored to be won by *juju* or magic, while early EO successes in Kono created an appearance of general effectiveness against the RUF. A discussion of EO's work and reputation can be found in Elizabeth Rubin, "An Army of One's Own," *Harper's* (February 1997): 44–55.

5. Interview with Colonel Andrew Gayle, Freetown, June 1998.

6. Abidjan Agreement, S/1996/1034.

7. The Abidjan Agreement were signed by President Henri Bedie of the Republic of the Côte d'Ivoire; Berhanu Dinka, special envoy of the UN Secretary-General for Sierra Leone; Adowa Coleman, representative of the Organization for African Unity; and Moses Anafu, representative of the Commonwealth Organization. Article 28 directs these institutions to stand as "moral guarantors that this Peace Agreement is implemented with integrity and in good faith by both parties." S/1996/1034, November 30, 1996.

8. See Abidjan Agreement, Article 3.

9. Interview with government official, December 22, 1997.

10. Confidential interview. For further discussion, see "War of Words Escalates," *Economist Intelligence Unit: Sierra Leone*, The Economist Group, London, May 1, 1997.

11. "Foday Sankoh Goes on Trial," *Economist Intelligence Unit: Sierra Leone*, January 29, 1999.

12. Sierra Leone Broadcasting Corporation, March 16, 1998. RUF's Phillip Palmer, in a press release, was quoted as saying that Sankoh's leadership had been terminated due to his "unyielding determination to thwart the peace process."

13. Interview with Desmond Luke, chairman of the Commission for the Consolidation of Peace, March 30, 1997.

14. Sierra Leone Broadcasting Corporation, May 25, 1997.

15. For reports alluding to this allegation, see FM 98.1 radio broadcasts (Pro-Democracy), "Sierra Leone News Update," January 9, 1998, available on Sierra Leone website: http://www.sierra-leone.org.

16. This was witnessed by U.S. Special Forces who were providing a three-week training program as described to the author.

17. AFRC Points for Negotiation, confidential document, May 30, 1997.

18. United Nations Secretariat, *Address to the Annual Assembly of Heads of State and Government of the Organization of African Unity,* Harare, June 2, 1997, SG/SM/6245 AFR/9.

19. Decision 356 of the Thirty-Third Summit of the Organization of African Unity (OAU) held in Harare, Zimbabwe, June 2–4, 1997, as found in United Nations, letter from the permanent representative of Guinea Bissau to the United Nations, addressed to the Secretary-General, September 18, 1997, A/52/465, October 16, 1997.

20. Ghana's active armed forces were composed of 5,000 army, 1,000 navy, and 1,000 air force personnel. Nigeria's active figures stood at 77,000 in 1997. These statistics are taken from the International Institute for Strategic Studies, *The Military Balance 1997/98* (Oxford: Oxford University Press, 1997).

21. Adebayo Oyebade, "Making Sierra Leone Safe for Democracy: Nigeria, ECOWAS and the May 25 Coup in Freetown," unpublished manuscript, pp. 9–10; ECOWAS, ECOWAS Foreign Ministers Communiqué, Conakry, June 27, 1997.

22. When the presidential election results were announced, the SLPP had won 36 percent of the votes while the next largest party, United National People's Party (UNPP), had 23 percent. The lack of a clear winner (needing 55 percent of the vote) required a second round wherein Kabbah (SLPP) won almost 60 percent and Karefa Smart (UNPP) received slightly more than 40 percent. Karefa Smart alleged election violations during the second round. Commonwealth, *Report of the Commonwealth Observer Group to the Presidential and Parliamentary Elections in Sierra Leone,* April 1996.

23. "In April 1999 the commander of ECOMOG in Sierra Leone, Maj.-Gen. Felix Mujakperuo, accused Burkina Faso of facilitating an illegal arms shipment to Revolutionary United Front (RUF) rebels in Sierra Leone in violation of the United Nations embargo. Speaking at a press conference in Freetown, he claimed that on March 14, 1999, a Ukrainian-registered cargo plane had delivered sixty-eight tons of weapons and ammunition to Ouagadougou. There, he alleged, the plane parked in the airport's VIP terminal and the weapons were transferred onto a plane destined for Liberia, which is also subject to a UN arms embargo, and then shipped onward to the RUF inside Sierra Leone. Mujakperou also reported the incident to the United Nations." From Human Rights Watch Letter to President Campaore (Burkina Faso Arms Inquiry Urged)—March 2000. Press release available online at www.hrw.org/press/2000/03/burkina0330press.htm.

24. ECOWAS, Statement of the ECOWAS Committee of Four, July 29–30, 1997. Available online at www.sierra-leone.org.

25. Government of Sierra Leone, "Address by H. E. Mr. Ahmad Tejan Kabbah, delivered at the meeting of heads of State of the Economic Community for West African States," Abuja, Nigeria, August 27, 1997. Available online at www.sierra-leone.org.

26. *Final Communiqué of the Summit of the Economic Community of West African States,* Abuja, August 28–29, 1997, S/1997/695, September 8, 1997.

27. See William Durch, "Keeping the Peace: Politics and Lessons of the 1990s," in William Durch (ed.), *UN Peacekeeping: American Policy and the Uncivil Wars of the 1990s* (New York: St. Martin's Press, 1996), pp. 1–34.

28. These efforts culminated in "The Millbrook Action Programme," issued by Commonwealth heads of government from their summit in Auckland, New Zealand, in 1995. For further discussion of the role of the UK and the Commonwealth Ministerial Action Group, see Commonwealth, "Commonwealth Proposes Further Measures Against Military Regime in Nigeria," *Currents,* no. 2 (1996).

29. United Nations Security Council, Statement by the President of the Security Council, July 11, 1997, S/PRST/1997/36.

30. United Nations Security Council, Resolution 1132, S/RES/1132 (1997), October 8, 1997.

31. ECOWAS, *ECOWAS Six-Month Peace Plan for Sierra Leone*, Conakry, October 23, 1997.

32. For reporting on the Nigerian victory, see Howard W. French, "Nigerians Take Capital of Sierra Leone as Junta Flees," *New York Times*, February 14, 1998.

33. See discussion of the Sierra Leone Selection Trust (SLST) in Chapter 1.

34. See "Mining Industry in Sierra Leone," *Mbendi Business Profile*, available at http://mbendi.co.za/indy/ming/mingsl.htm; Ian Douglas, "Fighting for Diamonds: Private Military Companies in Sierra Leone," in Jakkie Cilliers and Peggy Mason (eds.), *Peace, Profit, or Plunder: The Privatisation of Security in War-Torn African Societies* (Johannesburg, South Africa: Institute for Security Studies, Halfway House, 1999), pp. 175–200.

35. Several other actors were involved in discussions for reinstating the Kabbah government. *Africa Confidential*, "Chronology of Sierra Leone from 1991 to 1998: How Diamonds Fueled the Conflict," reports that several security groups offered their services, including Defence Systems Ltd. There were several interested financiers as well. *Africa Confidential* mentions Jean-Raymond Boulle as the CEO of American Mineral Fields, but Ian Douglas also reports that an Israeli entrepreneur was interested. The government, however, decided to stay with Saxena. Saxena's final contract allowed for "the right of the Grantee's internal security force to bear and use arms and an agreement regarding rules of engagement for such internal security force to be made with the Solicitor-General and Inspector General of Police." In return, Saxena was to pay the government $10 million. As cited in Ian Smillie, Lansana Gberie, and Ralph Hazelton, *The Heart of the Matter: Sierra Leone, Diamonds, and Human Security* (Toronto: Partnership Africa Canada, 2000), p. 57.

36. Marie Colvin and Nicholas Rufford, "Our Man in Sierra Leone Is the People's Hero," *The Times* (London), May 17, 1998, reported that the Memorandum of Understanding between Kabbah, Tim Spicer, and Rakesh Saxena stated: ". . . the Grantee [Saxena] agrees to give economic and other assistance, to the value of $10,000,000US to the Grantor [Kabbah] for . . . restoration of the Constitution."

37. Douglas, "Fighting for Diamonds," p. 190.

38. As described in Douglas, "Fighting for Diamonds," p. 192. He writes that the five-phase Sandline plan included the civil defense force as the lead element of the operation, with support from ECOMOG and coordination provided by Sandline communications and aircraft. Phase I involved isolating Bo and Kenema, Phase II required encircling key cities, Phase III simultaneous attacks, Phase IV the capturing of vital points, and Phase V, returning the Kabbah government.

39. *Africa Confidential* 39, no. 21 (October 23, 1998): "Militias and Market Forces."

40. Michael Jones, "Can Cook Beat Mercenaries?" *The Sunday Times* (London), May 17, 1998.

41. House of Commons, Select Committee on Foreign Affairs Minutes of Evidence, Appendix 5, Letter to Sir Thomas Legg from S. J. Berwin & Co, Solicitors to Mr. Tim Spicer, July 15, 1998, available online at http://www.publications.parliament.uk/pa/cm199899.

42. See Sir Thomas Legg, KCB,QC, and Sir Robin Ibbs, KBE, "Report of the Sierra Leone Arms Investigation" (London: The Stationery Office, July 27, 1998).

43. Jones, "Can Cook Beat the Mercenaries?"

4

Negotiating Peace

When President Kabbah returned to Freetown on March 10, 1998, there were high hopes that the Economic Community of West African States Cease-Fire Monitoring Group (ECOMOG) had succeeded in vanquishing the rebel forces.[1] The ten thousand–strong peacekeeping force was in control of Freetown and its environs, and the junta leaders of the Armed Forces Revolutionary Council (AFRC) and Revolutionary United Front (RUF) were on the run. Within two months, however, the RUF, with reportedly extensive external assistance from Liberia and Burkina Faso, reorganized, successfully evaded capture, and ultimately over the remainder of the year seized the military initiative.[2] While Sankoh was still in Nigerian custody, the core RUF field command based in Kailahun established lines of communication with other RUF and Sierra Leone Army (SLA) field commanders. Sam Bockarie, Dennis Mingo, and Gibril Massaquoi were in regular contact with each other, with S.A.J. Musa apparently playing a key role in organizing their strategy. In coordination with elements of the SLA led by Musa, the RUF carried out a series of hit-and-run attacks on remote villages and major towns in northern Sierra Leone. From March to June 1998, the International Committee of the Red Cross (ICRC) and Médecins sans Frontières (MSF) brought several hundred men, women, and children with amputated hands and arms to Freetown from remote villages in the north.[3] Conservative estimates are that these were no more than a quarter of all the people on whom these atrocities were inflicted; the rest presumably perished from their injuries.[4] By the end of 1998 the SLA and the RUF had wheeled back to the west, captured Makeni, and, in the last week of December, after capturing and destroying Hastings, they stood poised to reenter Freetown. As the security situation deteriorated, the United Nations and the few diplomatic missions remaining in Freetown evacuated most of their personnel. The SLA/RUF's attack on Freetown on January 6 was a major turning point, a reassertion of rebel staying power, a humiliation for

ECOMOG, and a profound setback for the government's efforts to persuade the population that the security situation was under control.

ECOMOG UNDER PRESSURE

Why did ECOMOG lose control of the situation? Three factors are particularly germane: change in leadership, insufficient logistics, and overextended responsibilities.

Leadership

The Nigerian army provided most of the senior command structure for ECOMOG operations in Liberia and Sierra Leone. Overall command of Sierra Leone operations initially was directed from ECOMOG headquarters in Monrovia, where the multinational peacekeepers were winding down their long involvement in the Liberian civil war.[5] When the coup took place in May 1997, ECOMOG force commander General Victor Malu sent Colonel (later Brigadier) Maxwell Khobe to take charge of ground opera-

Associated Press AP

Sierra Leone civilians are loaded onto a West African peacekeeper helicopter in Freetown, Sierra Leone, to be evacuated to neighboring Conakry, Guinea, Friday, January 8, 1999.

tions in Sierra Leone. Both men were notable for their dynamic hands-on leadership and forceful charismatic personalities.[6]

Khobe was in charge of ECOMOG ground operations in Sierra Leone from June 1997 to the ouster of the AFRC/RUF junta from Freetown nine months later. In Khobe's dramatic account, he and a small contingent of Nigerian soldiers landed by helicopter at Hastings just as the coup got under way. They immediately came under attack. For twelve days his unit was trapped by RUF snipers in the swampy flatlands on the eastern outskirts of the capital. Once Khobe's unit succeeded in breaking out, he crossed over to the Lungi peninsula and assumed command of Nigerian forces at the international airport, the vital link for reinforcements and resupply.[7] Over the following eight months Khobe, with Malu's support, pressed Abuja for additional manpower, building up the ECOMOG presence on the ground. Using Alpha jets operating from Monrovia, Nigerian pilots flew periodic sorties over Freetown. While the Economic Community of West African States (ECOWAS) pursued diplomatic efforts to persuade the junta to relinquish its control, Khobe prepared the strategy for the recapture of Freetown. In February 1998 he successfully coordinated the ground and air operation that, after a week of heavy fighting, forced the junta to retreat from Freetown.

However, shortly after Kabbah's return, there was a major change in the ECOMOG command structure. General Malu was transferred to Nigeria as director of the Army Staff College. The new commander for ECOMOG operations in Sierra Leone and Liberia was Major General Timothy Shelpidi. In May, Khobe, promoted to brigadier general, was reassigned as chief of the Defense Staff of the SLA, in effect becoming Kabbah's military adviser and removing him from responsibility for ECOMOG operations. In mid-June, Shelpidi moved his command from Monrovia to Freetown. In contrast to Khobe and Malu, Shelpidi's leadership proved lackluster and uninspiring. He spent most of his time in Freetown, failed to maintain direct contact with his troops in the field, and finally proved unable to prevent the RUF's reentry into Freetown. During the crucial three days of the SLA/RUF assault on Freetown (January 6–8, 1999), Shelpidi took President Kabbah across the estuary on a Nigerian naval ship to Lungi airport, and at least for some of that time was out of communication with his troops.[8]

Limited Logistics, Extended Responsibilities

Upon Kabbah's return to Freetown, ECOMOG assumed responsibility for carrying out the disarmament and demobilization of the Sierra Leone Army, maintaining law and order in Freetown and environs and pursuing the RUF. From the outset, ECOMOG was handicapped by insufficient resources and logistics. As long as Abacha was Nigerian head of state, potential donors apart from the United States maintained a hands-off policy toward ECOMOG. Additionally, the European Union and its member states had regulations restricting financial support for peacekeeping operations in Africa to those under United Nations command. The U.S. State Department's initial $3.9 million aid contract with Pacific Architects and Engineers and their subcontractor, International Charters Inc., to provide logistics assistance was barely sufficient to support six months of operations. Two Russian helicopters were brought in, and a fleet of eighty trucks donated by the government of the Netherlands was transferred from Monrovia to Freetown and Kenema. Pacific Architects and Engineers also established and ran maintenance depots in the two cities with the objective of keeping 80 percent of the vehicles on the road at any one time. Most of the money was quickly consumed by the high cost of the helicopter operations.

In the face of limited direct donor support, Nigeria was left to bear the principal financial burden. Nigeria claimed that its ECOMOG operations in Sierra Leone cost $1 million a day. However, there was neither transparency nor accountability in the disbursement of these funds. Inevitably, there was widespread speculation that some of the money intended to support ECOMOG never left Nigeria or was funneled to bank accounts of various military commanders. After Abacha's death his successor, General Abubakr, pursued a vigorous anticorruption campaign against a number of Nigerian military officers as well as Abacha's widow.[9]

ECOMOG VERSUS THE RUF: AN UNEVEN COMBAT

ECOMOG's lack of familiarity with the bush terrain of eastern Sierra Leone was as serious as its logistics problems. ECOMOG forces repeatedly fell prey to ambushes, fake surrenders, and surprise attacks. As their convoys became bogged down by fallen logs, trenches, or other devices to stop their advance, it became ever more difficult for the Nigerians to take the initiative. The Nigerian soldiers were ill-prepared to engage in hand-to-hand combat deep in the bush, but at the same time they were reluctant to develop too close a collaborative relationship with the Kamajohs, who had the experience and knowledge of RUF tactics that they lacked. The Nigerians kept Chief Norman at arm's length, asserting that the Kamajohs lacked the discipline and structure for effective combat operations. They probably also wanted to avoid involvement in Sierra Leone's internal politics. To a limited extent, ECOMOG used elements of the Sierra Leone Army who claimed restored allegiance to the government. But this sometimes proved to be a trap as well. On top of all these operational problems, some Nigerian soldiers also reportedly joined in the illegal diamond mining in the Kono region.[10]

ECOMOG's original plan was to seal off the Kailahun salient bordering Guinea and Liberia, which for the past seven years had been the RUF headquarters. In June, as the Nigerians advanced from the west, they were to be joined in a pincer movement by Guinean forces moving from the east. However, the Guinean units arrived late, enabling the rebel forces to break out and continue their attacks on remote villages in the north, encompassing a wide swath from Kono to Kambia, before turning back to Makeni and ultimately Freetown. The proof of SLA/RUF effectiveness was to be measured in the swelling population in the refugee camps across the border in Guinea. By the end of 1998 there were again 280,000 Sierra Leonean refugees in Guekedou and Fourekaria, the same total as three years earlier.[11] Northern Sierra Leone had become a zone of terror, a no-man's land. Neither ECOMOG nor the humanitarian agencies could operate freely, and the government's writ was virtually nonexistent. The RUF code-named their attacks "Operation No Living Thing," intended to convince the population that the government and ECOMOG were incapable of defending them.[12]

FROM ABACHA TO ABUBAKR

As these events transpired on the ground, the political situation was dramatically altered with the sudden death in Abuja of Nigerian head of state Sani Abacha in the early morning hours of June 8. Most African leaders, including President Kabbah, were attending an Organization of African Unity (OAU) summit meeting in Ouagadougou, Burkina Faso. In accordance with Muslim tradition, Abacha was buried before sundown the same day. Subsequently, there was widespread speculation that members of the Nigerian military command had arranged for him to be poisoned during the night by Indian prostitutes. Abacha had arrested General Diya, his second in command, several days earlier on charges of plotting a coup against him, and other arrests were expected.[13] Whatever the truth, Abacha's death immediately altered the Nigerian political scene. His successor, General Abdusalam Abubakr, promptly announced his intention to hold elections within a year for the restoration of civilian government.[14] President Kabbah went directly from Ouagadougou to northern Nigeria to express condolences to Abacha's widow. Aware of the profound implications for Sierra Leone, Kabbah obtained Abubakr's promise that Nigerian forces would remain in Sierra Leone until peace and security were assured. But the prospect of a civilian government inevitably changed the political dynamic in the region, raising the prospect of a reduction and ultimately withdrawal of Nigerian forces sooner rather than later. This in turn increased the pressure for a negotiated settlement with the RUF.

THE GOVERNMENT IN DISARRAY

Upon its return, the government was unable to capitalize on public enthusiasm and found itself severely constrained by lack of resources. Its regained popularity quickly dissipated as it failed to deliver fundamental services. The ministers returned from exile to looted offices, destroyed homes, and empty coffers. A number of ministers and other senior officials lived for several months in the Cape Sierra Hotel, either gratis or courtesy of the Nigerian government. State House, the office of the president in the center of Freetown, had been severely damaged, and was virtually abandoned except for a few offices. Ministers in most cases lacked transportation and had to hitch rides to get to meetings. Under these circumstances it is not surprising that the government was unable to deliver basic services. There was also a perception, fairly or otherwise, that some ministers were more interested in securing contracts from the international community's involvement in the disarmament and demobilization program than in running their ministries.

The medical sector was completely dependent on supplies from international NGOs and the United Nations. The few Sierra Leonean doctors and nurses left in the country, together with teams from MSF and ICRC, struggled valiantly to deal with the enormous caseload of amputees arriving in Makeni and Freetown. At Connaught Hospital a small team of surgeons worked tirelessly to save the lives of the victims of RUF brutality. For several months, MSF-funded helicopter flights were organized to bring the survivors to Freetown. There was virtually no capacity, however, for dealing with the psychological trauma of these injuries. Several hundred amputees were moved to a makeshift camp at Hastings, from where the many pictures of women and small children with severed arms and legs were transmitted around the world by Cable Network News (CNN) and other media. It was a major factor in gaining international attention for the ongoing crisis. But the attention to the amputees only veiled the prevalence of the myriad of other diseases, including malaria, tuberculosis, and AIDS, that afflicted a population suffering severe poverty and malnutrition as well.

The school year had been extended to August (after classes had been suspended during the period of junta rule), but the educational system, reeling from years of neglect and corruption, was barely functioning. Many teachers had fled abroad. Those who remained behind found payment of salaries delayed by insufficient resources and arguments over "ghost" teachers still on the government payrolls. Books and other materials were in short supply. When I visited the minister of education in his office in June 1999, he was barricaded behind window grates. He explained that this was protection against angry teachers, not the RUF.

President Kabbah, on the basis of security considerations and temperamentally averse to public appearances, became a virtual recluse in Freetown, although he attended international meetings in New York and London. His office in the renovated former residence of the colonial British governor general (paid for by the Nigerians), high up on the central spine of hills curving around the western side of the city, effectively cut him off from public view. In near seclusion, the president received visitors and spoke periodically on the radio. Aside from a brief visit to Connaught Hospital with Jesse Jackson and U.S. ambassador Joseph Melrose in mid-November and a few other events, he was rarely seen in public. More seriously, perhaps, the cabinet met only sporadically while the parliament was largely marginalized. After the near SLA/RUF takeover of the capital in January 1999, the specific issue of how security around the capital had collapsed or what could be done to avert its happening again was never discussed by the legislature. *WHY ? THIS SEEMS VERY IMPT !*

discourage team military The one partial achievement of this period was the start, albeit limited, of demobilization. Several thousand Sierra Leonean army officers and soldiers had turned themselves over to ECOMOG.[15] Kabbah decided that 750 of them would be allowed to stay in the army despite vociferous parliamentary objections. The others were encamped at various locations around the capital as well as at Lungi airport partially for their own protection. In any case, without sufficient resources the long-delayed disarmament and demobilization program remained limited in scope. In June 1999 the first 250 soldiers were demobilized in a formal ceremony. In the meantime, the Nigerians began training the first 84 soldiers of what was to be the new Sierra Leone army. Clearly this was going to be a slow process. *laying down arms esp: reduction of nations military forces*

THE TREASON TRIALS

The government, responding to popular anger, focused its efforts on organizing three sets of treason trials that took their course throughout the summer and fall. As the RUF had evaded capture, the brunt of these proceedings fell on officers and soldiers of the SLA as well as members of the civil service who were charged with collaborating with the junta. In April, fifty-nine AFRC civilians, including former president Momoh, cabinet ministers, parliamentarians, and pro-junta journalists, were charged with treason; some were also charged with murder and arson. By November 4 the three trials had concluded with convictions and death sentences imposed on forty-seven of the defendants. Former president Momoh and four others received lesser sentences; seven defendants were acquitted. The death sentences were appealed and ultimately not carried out.

Less fortunate were twenty-four out of thirty-four military officers tried under separate court-martial proceedings. They included former chief of Defense Staff Hassan Conteh and Chief of Army Staff Max Kanga, as well as one woman, Major Kula Samba, who had served as the junta's minister of social welfare. President Kabbah exercised his prerogative under the constitution to commute the death penalty on ten officers, but there was no internationally accepted appeals process for the others. The twenty-four officers were summarily executed by a Sierra Leonean firing squad accompanied by ECOMOG troops just before dawn on October 19. President Kabbah explained in a radio address the same morning that the officers had shown no remorse for their actions and in some cases indicated that given the opportunity they would act again. Amnesty International and other human rights organizations condemned the executions as a significant violation of human rights conventions, asserting that the court-martial itself was unfair and that the officers had not been given the opportunity to appeal their convictions to an independent tribunal.[16] There was, however, little adverse outcry in Freetown.

While these trials proceeded, the most dramatic event was the return from Nigeria on July 25 of RUF leader Foday Sankoh to Freetown to stand trial for treason. For security reasons Sankoh was kept at an undisclosed and carefully guarded location apart from the civilian AFRC defendants held in Pademba Road Prison. Before his trial began, Sankoh spoke on Sierra Leone television and radio in handcuffs alongside Information Minister Julius Spencer to appeal for an end to the fighting. Sankoh said he had never ordered atrocities against civilians and called upon his followers to cease their attacks on rural villages and to participate in the disarmament and demobilization process. RUF field commander Sam Bockarie, however, questioned whether Sankoh was speaking freely, and indicated that the RUF would continue its attacks.[17]

Sankoh's trial got under way in early October. Sankoh insisted on representing himself, but the government continued to try to find defense counsel. However, when it proved impossible to find a Sierra Leonean attorney to act as his defense lawyer, government efforts focused on the selection of a British barrister. The appointment, however, was only confirmed after his conviction.[18] At the trial, Sankoh spoke on his own behalf, maintaining that the Abidjan Agreement provided amnesty for his followers and himself. On October 23, 1999, Sankoh was convicted on seven of nine counts of treason after less than two hours of deliberation by a twelve-person jury. It was four days after the summary executions noted above.

High Court Justice Samuel Ademosu said in sentencing him to death: "Had you not given the order for your rebels to come out of the bush and join forces with the AFRC the atrocities could have been averted."[19] Sankoh's lawyer immediately appealed the conviction. It was to be one of the bitter ironies of the situation that Sankoh was to escape execution, as would all his RUF associates, while the brunt of the ultimate punishment fell only on the officers of the Sierra Leone Army.

Sankoh was remanded to Pademba Road Prison, where, as was the case for all condemned prisoners, he wore a T-shirt with the letter *C* emblazoned on it. As the appeal process languished, the political and security environment changed. While the government never said so directly, by the beginning of 1999 Sankoh became more useful alive than dead for the flagging peace process. Sankoh remained in jail until mid-March when he was allowed to go to Lomé, Togo, but his execution was no longer an issue.

TOWARD THE CEASE-FIRE

After the SLA/RUF January assault on Freetown and the near defeat of ECOMOG, the government found itself in a weakened diplomatic position. The government's key supporters—Nigeria, the United Kingdom, and the United States—believed the time was ripe for another effort at mediation. President Kabbah spent time alone with Sankoh and subsequently told this writer and others that he believed Sankoh had had a change of heart and was now ready for peace.[20] Sankoh, while still on death row, was taken quietly on a tour of the eastern part of the city, and reportedly expressed regret for the damage and suffering inflicted on the population. When UN Envoy Okelo and Togolese foreign minister Joseph Koffigoh met him in Conakry at the end of January, however, Sankoh claimed he could not agree to a cease-fire as long as he remained a prisoner condemned to death. During this meeting, Sankoh defiantly wore his prison uniform even though he was offered civilian dress. Subsequently, after discussions with President Kabbah, and separately with Ambassador Melrose, perhaps due to indications that his prisoner status would be suspended, Sankoh indicated privately that he was ready to accede to a cease-fire as a first step toward negotiating a new peace agreement.

In a pattern that repeated itself over the next months, the RUF sought to take advantage of ECOWAS's setback. They insisted that Sankoh—still condemned to death—be allowed to go to Mali or Togo for consultations with his commanders. The government's proposal to negotiate the terms of the cease-fire on a British ship offshore from Freetown was promptly rejected. Finally, Kabbah agreed over cabinet objections to allow Sankoh to go to Lomé, Togo. Some ministers wanted to delay the cease-fire to allow more time for ECOMOG to pursue RUF forces, and thus weaken the RUF's negotiating position. However, U.S. special envoy for democracy in Africa Jesse Jackson, on his way to the African-American summit in Accra, called Kabbah in Freetown and persuaded him to go with him from Accra to Lomé, where the cease-fire was signed on May 18. Kabbah went to Lomé without his key advisers, James Jonah and Solomon Berewa, for whom there was no space in the helicopter, creating the perception that Jackson forced Kabbah to agree to the ceasefire against his will. Actually, as noted above, Kabbah agreed with his international supporters that this was a new opportunity for peace.

CIVIL SOCIETY SEEKS TO PRESERVE DEMOCRACY

For the democratic forces, the Lomé [banishing or excluding] negotiations were a bitter and painful reversal from the international ostracism of the RUF almost two years earlier. With the government's major international supporters determined to press for a settlement, civil society had little ability to alter the situation or even to slow down the pace of negotiations. In June, Kabbah convened a National Consultative Conference in Freetown bringing together a broad range of civil-society actors ostensibly [apparently] to help determine the government's position. The president preempted the discussion in his opening remarks, insisting that the government would not agree either to a national unity government or to a power-sharing arrangement with the RUF. The rebels would be allowed to form a political party and compete in the next general election. This stance would be overridden in Lomé when the government drew a fine distinction between power sharing as constituting a new government and the RUF's participation in the elected government (subject to post facto registration for the election they had boycotted and parliamentary approval of ministerial nominations). For many Sierra Leoneans, it was ultimately a distinction without a difference.

The Regional Politics of the Lomé Negotiations

The Lomé negotiations got under way on May 25, four days before the inauguration of Olusegun Obasanjo, Nigeria's first democratically elected president in sixteen years. With Abacha's death, the ECOWAS chairmanship had passed first to Abubakr and then to Togolese president Gnassingbe Eyadema. Both Nigeria and Togo had a major stake in the outcome. Nigeria's position as the regional hegemon with the most troops on the ground in Sierra Leone would be central to implementation of the agreement. While Obasanjo repeated Abubakr's pledge not to withdraw Nigerian forces until peace was assured, in his election campaign he undertook to review Nigeria's military role in Sierra Leone. By his inauguration, he was already encountering strong domestic pressures for troop reductions.[21] Eyadema, in office since 1967, had repeatedly been criticized in the West for his poor human rights record.[22] With personalized head-of-state politics still the norm in West Africa, he clearly wanted to garner the credit for a peace settlement. When Kabbah stopped in Tripoli, Libya, in mid-June en route back from a state visit to China, Libyan president, Colonel Muammar Qaddafi, offered to mediate directly if Eyadema would enable his now-famous guest rebel leader to travel. Eyadema refused, unwilling to allow Qaddafi to get the credit for brokering the peace agreement at his expense.[23]

The Role of the Regional and International Facilitators

Togolese foreign minister Joseph Koffigoh, on behalf of ECOWAS, and UN Special Envoy Okelo steered the forty-five days of negotiations, with OAU and Commonwealth representatives also present. U.S. ambassador Joseph Melrose and Paul Harvey from the Foreign Office in London played important behind-the-scenes roles in informal consultations with the parties. The initial presence of former Libyan permanent representative to the United Nations Ali Trieki, and later of the Libyan ambassador to Togo, reflected Libya's renewed interest in being perceived as an African peacemaker. Although not in attendance, Obasanjo and Taylor also were to have a major impact on the outcome. The Sierra Leone Inter-Religious Council, as well as several civil-society groups, were allowed to sit in at the formal negotiating sessions. They sought to establish an informal dialogue with the RUF. According to one participant, the RUF expressed concerns about the danger of retribution.[24]

Koffigoh and Okelo saw their role as assisting the two sides in working out a viable agreement that would get Sierra Leone off the agenda of Africa's intractable conflicts. After eight years of war and massive destruction, they viewed the talks as the last chance to save the country from total collapse. In comparison with the Abidjan negotiations three years earlier, relations between the government and the RUF were reversed to a large extent. In 1996 the government with the support of Executive Outcomes and the Kamajohs had brought the RUF close to defeat. Sankoh had come to Abidjan to buy time and gain a respite. President Kabbah's standing was high as the leader of a newly elected democratic government. By 1999, in contrast, Sankoh was in the stronger position given the inability of ECOWAS to defeat the RUF. While the RUF could not get all it wanted, it was clear to all parties that a renewed ECOMOG military offensive was not an option the international community would support. Kabbah, worn down and weakened by the coup, the siege of Freetown, and his dependence on the Nigerians, offered Sankoh the chairmanship of a Commission for the Management of Strategic Resources, National Reconstruction, and Development. As one Western diplomat succinctly summarized the situation, "Kabbah wanted peace, Sankoh wanted power."[25]

At home, Kabbah faced an imminent cabinet revolt as a number of ministers criticized the president's personal diplomatic style, and questioned his optimism that Sankoh had become a convert to peace and reconciliation. The hard-liners were convinced that it was only a matter of time before the accord would break down or the RUF's designs on the presidency would be fulfilled. The fact that Kabbah kept the details of the negotiating process to himself only fueled their anxieties. The president in turn contended that these concerns were the understandable consequence of the trauma the nation had suffered. But he stuck to his conviction that a peace deal could work.[26] When he finally presented the agreement to the cabinet, they acceded and voted for its approval. From an outsider's perspective, they had no choice.

THE LOMÉ NEGOTIATIONS

In the two years following the May 1997 coup the RUF had further developed its regional and international networks. In addition to continuing support from Liberia, Burkina Faso, and perhaps Libya, a number of Sierra Leonean politicians abroad were ready to form ad hoc coalitions with the rebels. Among these were Omrie Golley, a British-trained lawyer, and former UN permanent representative Pallo Bangura ("foreign minister" in the AFRC/RUF junta), who formed the RUF negotiating team, which also included several field commanders. Sankoh himself did not take part in the negotiations but, as in Abidjan two and a half years earlier, spent his time granting interviews and living well with his latest companions in one of Lomé's most luxurious hotels.

The RUF started with a maximalist position, demanding a four-year transitional government of national unity and the appointment of Sankoh as vice president.[27] The government delegation led by Attorney General Solomon Berewa held open the possibility of several cabinet seats while rejecting the demand for the vice presidency. The RUF would be allowed to become a political party and run in the next election in 2001. As the talks continued, the RUF pressed for major portfolios: foreign affairs, finance, defense, or justice. After considerable haggling, it was agreed that the RUF would be given four cabinet posts and four deputy-ministerial positions, all subject to parliamentary approval. After the two sides agreed in principle on these terms and a blanket amnesty, Sankoh insisted that the negotiators consult his senior commander, Sam Bockarie, and other field commanders

Associated Press AP

Sierra Leone's President Ahmed Tejan Kabbah, right, sits with rebel Revolutionary United Front leader Foday Sankoh at a dinner for heads of state arriving for peace talks in Lomé, Togo, Tuesday, July 6, 1999.

still operating inside Sierra Leone before the RUF could give its formal agreement. A delegation including Koffigoh traveled into the bush. Bockarie pressed for three additional seats but, reportedly at Charles Taylor's intercession, these demands were dropped. Amidst considerable fanfare, Kabbah and Sankoh signed the agreement in Lomé on July 7, in the presence of a panoply of regional leaders.[28]

The Lomé Peace Agreement's thirty-seven articles and five annexes in many aspects replicated the Abidjan Agreement.[29] The agreement included a renewed commitment to an end to hostilities; reestablishment of the Commission for the Consolidation of Peace; provisions for demobilization, disarmament, and reintegration into civil society of all combatants; and the transformation of the RUF into a political party. It requested the UN Observer Mission in Sierra Leone (UNOMSIL) and ECOMOG to jointly comprise a neutral peacekeeping force, and called for the recruitment and training of a new Sierra Leone Army and the withdrawal of all mercenaries.

The new elements included the above-noted positions in a broad-based government of national unity, and the establishment of the Commission for the Management of Strategic Resources, National Reconstruction, and Development (Article V). Sankoh was offered the commission chairmanship with "the status of Vice President" for this purpose and "therefore answerable only to the President."[30]   *(general pardon granted by a govt esp.) for political offenses*

The provisions in Article IX for pardon and amnesty, which later proved highly controversial, were apparently accepted with little discussion. They included (1) the "absolute and free pardon and reprieve to all combatants and collaborators in respect of anything done by them in pursuit of their objectives" and (2) the undertaking that "no official or judicial action is taken against any member of the RUF/SL, ex-AFRC, ex-SLA or CDF in respect of anything done by them in pursuit of their objectives as members of these organizations"[31] from March 1991 to the date of signing of the agreement. The blanket amnesty clearly was a core requirement of the RUF before it would sign the agreement. Similar language in the Abidjan Agreement had not raised a hue and cry, probably because the international community (other than the immediate negotiators) had little interest in or awareness of what was happening in Sierra Leone.

This time, in contrast, Kabbah's willingness to agree to the blanket amnesty raised major concerns for the newly appointed United Nations High Commissioner for Human Rights, Mary Robinson, and the international human rights community.[32] Okelo was initially instructed from UN headquarters not to sign the agreement. Okelo remonstrated, noting that the   *(pleaded in protest or objection)* entire agreement would collapse absent his signature. He was then instruct-   *(warning, caution, explanation)* ed to append a handwritten caveat that the United Nations does not acknowledge the application of this amnesty to "acts of genocide, crimes against humanity, war crimes and other serious violations of international humanitarian law."[33] The blanket amnesty also cast in doubt the establishment of the Truth and Reconciliation Commission envisaged in Article XXVI "to address impunity, [and] break the cycle of violence."[34] On a visit to eastern Freetown and Hastings the week before the Lomé agreement was concluded, residents told this writer they were prepared to accept the amnesty as long as the war was truly at an end.[35] It was a view that seemed to have wide resonance among a war-weary population.

add as a supplement or appendix

THE COLLAPSE OF THE PEACE AGREEMENT

The attitude of many participants at Lomé was summed up by one Western observer with the question "What is the choice?" ECOWAS was no longer prepared to assist the Kabbah government in seeking a military solution. President Obasanjo was under domestic pressure to bring the conflict to a close and draw down Nigeria's long-standing troop presence. The toll of Nigerian casualties as well as the costs, coupled with the dire official budgetary picture after years of state corruption, were major considerations for the new president. The United Kingdom and the United States also had

Memuna Mansaray, 3, whose right arm was destroyed by terrorist rebels, plays with her brother Ibrahim, 9, at the Camp for War Wounded and Amputees, in Freetown, Sierra Leone, Wednesday, September 1, 1999.

concluded that the only responsible way forward was a negotiated political settlement.[36] The Lomé agreement, by giving the RUF a role in governance and legalized access to mineral wealth, was seen as the best chance for peace. At the same time, a Joint Implementation Committee (Article XXXII) composed of the CCP, the ECOWAS Committee of Seven, and the other moral guarantors, to meet at least once every three months, was intended to provide the oversight that had been absent from the Abidjan Accords. That said, the effectiveness of these arrangements clearly depended on the intentions of the RUF and its regional supporters, especially Liberia. Initial signs that the agreement would hold included Sankoh's public declaration of support for President Kabbah.[37] But early euphoria had characterized other moments of transition (the National Provisional Ruling Council accession to power; the 1996 election; the Abidjan Agreement) only to be replaced by disillusionment.

By December 1999 it was clear that the peace process was in trouble; Sierra Leone remained divided between areas under ECOMOG and RUF control. The disarmament process was barely under way with at most 10,000 of the estimated 45,000 combatants presenting themselves at demobilization centers.[38] These were mostly from the Sierra Leone Army.

Sankoh publicly endorsed the government's call for disarmament while his second in command, Sam Bockerie, still in the field, defiantly announced that his men would not disarm. Some observers in Freetown thought this was a deliberate "good cop, bad cop" ruse designed to drag out the process while diamond mining continued feverishly in the east. There was also speculation that Nigerian commanders were in no rush to proceed with disarmament for the same reason. On December 21, in a meeting with Taylor and Obasanjo in Monrovia, Bockarie was given an "ECOWAS order" not to return to Sierra Leone until disarmament was completed and the next elections took place. He was nominally sent into exile for eighteen months.[39]

The international community's rhetorical support for Lomé quickly proved far greater than its tangible commitments.[40] If the RUF was to be persuaded to disarm, the financial and material resources for disarmament and peacekeeping needed to be quickly available. But the Lomé agreement was signed as major donors focused their attention on identifying resources for Kosovo and East Timor. The financial backing to fully implement Lomé's disarmament and demobilization provisions was unavailable, although the United Kingdom did provide 20 million pounds to the UN Trust Fund.

The Lomé agreement led to a significantly strengthened United Nations presence in Sierra Leone. The Security Council voted on October 22 (Resolution 1270) to establish the United Nations Mission in Sierra Leone (UNAMSIL) as a peacekeeping force of up to 6,000 troops including 260 unarmed observers.[41] Acting under Chapter VII of the UN Charter the peacekeepers were authorized "to take the necessary measures . . . to afford protection to civilians under imminent threat of physical violence."[42] The initial force included troops from countries already contributing to ECOMOG: Ghana, Guinea, and Nigeria, to which were added Indian and Kenyan contingents. In October, Major General Vijay Kumar Jetley of India was named as force commander. Subsequently in mid-December, Ole Adeniji, a senior Nigerian diplomat, succeeded Francis Okelo as UN Special Envoy, a move intended to signal Nigeria's continued commitment to the peace process. Nigeria reversed its initial concept of parallel UN and ECOMOG commands, agreeing to provide four battalions to an expanded UNAMSIL as its ECOMOG contingents were drawn down. Acting on the Secretary-General's recommendation, the Security Council voted on February 7, 2000 (Resolution 1289), to enlarge UNAMSIL to 11,100 troops. Its mandate under Chapter VII was expanded to include provision of security at key locations in and near Freetown, and at all disarmament sites.[43]

UNAMSIL was faced by major challenges from the start as efforts to expand its areas of deployment to the north and east precipitated confrontations with the RUF. In January–February 2000, RUF forces refused to present themselves at assigned disarmament locations. Instead, RUF elements confronted small numbers of UNAMSIL troops at isolated locations. In one particularly glaring incident, a small band of RUF fighters forced over a hundred Guinean troops to surrender their weapons and vehicles. Sankoh's responses varied from disingenuous denials of responsibility to broad reassertion of the RUF's commitment to the disarmament process.[44] In effect, Sankoh replayed his well-honed tactic of constantly moving the goalposts, demanding more resources before disarmament proceeded, and ultimately asserting that the UN should not be in Sierra Leone at all.

Two Weeks in May

The dramatic events of May 2000 brought to the fore all the doubts and foreboding about the RUF's intentions. On May 1, a major new crisis erupted. With the final departure of ECOMOG troops, Sankoh apparently decided that the RUF could advance its agenda of intimidation and control of the diamond areas unhindered. Opposed to UNAMSIL deployment into the diamond fields of Kono and Tongo, the RUF seized close to five hundred Kenyan and Zambian peacekeepers in remote locations in the north and east. This time, however, Sankoh miscalculated the consequences for himself, his followers, and the future of the Lomé peace process.

In London, the Blair government quickly decided to undertake a major military operation. Amidst reports that RUF rebels were preparing to re-enter Freetown, Britain moved to mount an evacuation of British and other foreign nationals. The massive deployment also included a broader objective. Seven hundred paratroopers arrived to restore security in and around the capital, and to bolster the morale and resolve of the UN peacekeepers. Seven Royal Navy warships with a fleet of helicopters and jet aircraft anchored offshore to provide logistical support and air-combat capability. It was the largest British expeditionary force since the Falklands war in 1982. Their presence was clearly a major psychological boost for the battered population.

While UNAMSIL forces regrouped into more defensible positions, Secretary-General Annan approached Qaddafi and Taylor to assist in negotiations for release of the peacekeepers. Over the ensuing ten days, Taylor, the only regional leader who had direct contact with the RUF, interceded to facilitate the phased release of virtually all the peacekeepers except for the six reported killed.[45] In Abuja, ECOWAS military chiefs endorsed President Obasanjo's decision to send as many as three thousand additional Nigerian troops to bolster UNAMSIL's strength. In a May 19 statement, the government called for the RUF to release all UN peacekeepers and abductees, cease attacks on government and UNAMSIL forces, withdraw from Kono, and immediately renew the disarmament process.[46]

In New York, Secretary-General Annan and his senior associates had to respond simultaneously to the hostage crisis and the media perception of another botched United Nations peacekeeping mission. The humiliation of the captured Kenyan and Zambian peacekeepers was seen as reminiscent of Mladic's treatment of the Dutch UN Protection Force battalion at Srebenica. Special Envoy Adeniji and General Jetley were charged with misjudging Sankoh's actions and intentions, erroneously convincing themselves that they could work with him and obtain his adherence to Lomé's disarmament provisions.[47] UN peacekeepers, it was asserted, were again trying to maintain a peace that did not exist. The Security Council, especially the United States, was criticized for deploying peacekeepers without adequate equipment and logistics into what had become an untenable mission.[48] The United States and the United Kingdom were accused of forcing Kabbah to sign the Lomé Peace Agreement, specifically including the blanket amnesty that made the RUF immune from prosecution.[49]

UNAMSIL's severe difficulties and setbacks, reminiscent of earlier crises in Somalia and Rwanda, again underscored the futility of deploying peacekeeping forces with inadequate resources, equipment, and logistics. Responsibility clearly fell in the first instance on the permanent members of the Security Council, who control and determine its decisions. Five years after the *Agenda for Peace,* the UN Secretariat still needed to find a way to manage and direct complex peacekeeping operations.[50] This included the clear need for a significantly improved intelligence capability, strong field leadership, and appropriately equipped and supported troops. The examples of United Nations peace operations in Korea in 1950 and Desert Storm in 1991 proved that Chapter VII enforcement operations could work provided there was strong leadership as well as resources and logistics in support of a coherent and sustainable strategy.

Exeunt Sankoh

In Freetown a massive civil society protest demonstration was organized on May 8 demanding the release of the peacekeepers. UN Special Envoy Olu Adeniji and Libyan envoy Ali Treiki had urged Kabbah to dissuade the leadership from proceeding to Sankoh's house, fully aware of the potential for violence. It was too late. An estimated thirty thousand people approached Sankoh's house on Spur Road. As they pressed forward, one of the Nigerian peacekeepers shot in the air. When people continued to surge forward, Sankoh's bodyguards started firing indiscriminately into the crowd. The Nigerian soldiers were overwhelmed and lost control of the situation. When it was over, seventeen civilians were dead and dozens more injured. In the panic and confusion, Sankoh escaped over a back wall in women's clothing. The house was ransacked. A massive funeral in Freetown's stadium on May 12 for those killed in the violence made it clear that the public held Sankoh personally responsible for the deaths.

Early on May 17, Sankoh was found near his residence and was captured by a Sierra Leonean soldier. After being stripped and paraded naked in the streets, he was placed under government custody and taken by a British helicopter to an undisclosed location near Lungi Airport.

After nine months of negotiating Sankoh's inclusion in the Lomé process, his arrest brought about an abrupt turn in the situation. The RUF's attacks on United Nations forces, continued grip on the diamond fields, and refusal to commit to a time frame for disarmament made clear that Sankoh's acceptance of the peace agreement, once again, was only tactical. Documents taken from Sankoh's residence revealed his flagrant disregard of the Lomé Peace Agreement's ban on illegal diamond mining. They showed that following his return to Freetown in October 1999, he was continuing to systematically exploit the country's diamonds for his personal benefit. Sankoh kept meticulous records showing that he had personally received two thousand stones of varying sizes that he was trying to sell in Antwerp.[51]

A broad consensus at the UN and ECOWAS quickly developed, holding Sankoh directly responsible for the May 8 fatalities. Taylor's efforts to arrange his removal to a third country were quickly rebuffed. On May 26, President Kabbah announced that Sankoh would be put on trial under Sierra Leonean law. In a June 16 letter to Secretary-General Annan, President Kabbah requested that the Security Council establish a special court for Sierra Leone that would prosecute "the most responsible violators and the leadership of the RUF" under a combination of international and domestic law for war crimes and crimes against humanity.[52]

By the end of June 2000, the international community and the Kabbah government faced the stark reality that the decade of war was not yet over. For all practical purposes, the Lomé Peace Agreement had collapsed. The Security Council moved toward a new strategy encompassing (1) a further increase in UNAMSIL troop strength, (2) establishment of a special court to prosecute Sankoh and others on the Arusha or Cambodian model, and (3) an embargo on diamonds from Sierra Leone. These steps were, however, only pieces of the picture. The Lomé agreement's disarmament provisions needed to be preserved. As one observer put it, RUF fighters needed to see a potential civilian future for themselves if they were not to return to the forest.[53] Finally, Taylor's role emerged, more clearly than ever, as pivotal. As long as Liberia sought access to Sierra Leone's diamonds and offered refuge to RUF fighters, the war would continue. As one Security Council ambassador put it, UNAMSIL was in effect being asked to solidify the par-

[handwritten margin note: Being of vital impt. or crucial]

tition of the country. Despite a massive international effort, it was clear that stabilization and reconstruction of Sierra Leone would be a long time in coming.

NOTES

1. "I urgently looked for help from friendly countries and organisations, particularly ECOWAS, to rescue you and our country from the hands of those mutinous rabbles and their collaborators. It is with a deep sense of gratitude that I say to you that ECOMOG came at once to our rescue on being mandated to do so. As you have seen, it is because of the high professionalism of these magnificent men and the gallant efforts of our Civil Defence Forces that we are here today to restart our lives." Government of Sierra Leone, Address to the Nation by His Excellency The President of Sierra Leone, Alhaji Dr. Ahmad Tejan Kabbah, at the Siaka Stevens Stadium, Freetown, on Tuesday, March 10, 1998. Available online at www.sierra-leone.org.

2. Accusations against Liberia and Burkina Faso as well as Libya are common. For sample press coverage of allegations, see Africa News Service, "ECOWAS Summit: Liberian Faction Accused of Meddling in Sierra Leone," October 31, 1998; Inter-Press Service, "Politics: Sierra Leone: Exposing the Hidden Hand of Libya," October 19, 1998; and Lansana Fofana, "Libya Funded Sierra Leone's Civil War, Court Hears," *Mail and Guardian*, October 16, 1998. More recent news articles include: "Burkina Faso Denies Arming Rebels," BBC News, May 19, 2000; United Nations Office for the Coordination of Humanitarian Affairs, IRIN, "Sierra Leone: Cook Points to Liberia-RUF Diamond Connection," June 7, 2000; Mike Donkin, "Liberia: Where Rebels Roam Free," BBC News, June 14, 2000; and Douglas Farah, "Liberia Reportedly Arming Guerillas," *Washington Post*, June 18, 2000.

3. Medecins Sans Frontieres, *Report: Overview of the Sierra Leone Crisis— the Humanitarian Situation Known to MSF*, Brussels, July 1998.

4. Author's interview with MSF field staff Martha Carey and Monique Nagelkerk, Freetown, April 1998.

5. See Robert Mortimer, "From ECOMOG to ECOMOG II: Intervention in Sierra Leone," in John W. Harbeson and Donald Rothchild (eds.), *Africa in World Politics: The African State System in Flux*, 3d Edition (Boulder, CO: Westview Press, 2000), pp. 188–207.

6. General Victor Malu and Maxwell Khobe had significant experience from lessons learned in Operation Octopus in Liberia. For Khobe's background, see Xinhua, "ECOMOG Chief in Control of Sierra Leone Internal Security," April 16, 1998, and Africa News Service, "Meet Nigerian Col. Khobe, ECOMOG Strongman," April 16, 1998.

7. Author's interview with Colonel Khobe, Freetown, June 1998.

8. Author's confidential interview with a member of the Sierra Leone cabinet, June 1999.

9. "Large-Scale Official Corruption Is Outlined," *Economist Intelligence Unit: Nigeria*, February 4, 1999; and "Opening Up Aso Rock," *Africa Confidential* 39, no. 18 (September 11, 1998): 2.

10. To see press reports of allegations, see Agence France-Presse, "ECOMOG Preventing End of War Due to Diamonds," October 26, 1998.

11. UN High Commissioner for Refugees, "Refugee Population by Country of Asylum and Origin, 1997–1998," *Refugees and Others of Concern to UNHCR— 1998 Statistical Overview* (Geneva: UNHCR, 1998). By 1999, Sierra Leonean refugees outnumbered Guinean nationals in Gueckdou area as cited in Human Rights Watch, *Forgotten Children of War: Sierra Leonean Refugee Children in Guinea*, vol. 11, no. 5, July 1999.

12. As quoted in testimony in Human Rights Watch, *Sierra Leone: Sowing Terror—Atrocities Against Civilians in Sierra Leone*, vol. 10, no. 3, July 1998.

13. "Government Urged to Release Coup Plot Convicts," *Economist Intelligence Unit: Nigeria*, February 4, 1999.

14. Marcus Mabry and Joshua Hammer, "Nigerian Roulette," *Newsweek*, June 22, 1998.

15. Sullay Sesay of the National Committee for Disarmament, Demobilization, and Reintegration cited a government estimate of 33,000 excombatants by July 1999. Of these 25,000 were in the Civil Defense Force (CDF), 7,000 from the SLA, and 1,000 in the RUF. Before the signing of the Peace Agreement in July, 2,974 soldiers were participating in the Disarmament, Demobilization, and Reintegration (DDR) program. UN Office for the Coordination of Humanitarian Affairs, "Sierra Leone: IRIN Special Report on Demobilization," July 9, 1999.

16. Amnesty International, *Sierra Leone 1998—A Year of Atrocities Against Civilians*, AF 51/22/98, London, November 1998.

17. BBC Focus on Africa, "Interview with Sam Bockarie," October 20, 1998.

18. Inter-Press Service, "No Lawyer Willing to Defend Rebel Leader," September 8, 1998. The British barrister was former minister Douglas Hogg; also chosen was London-based lawyer Charles Buckley. These lawyers were chosen in part because their services would be paid by an international human rights organization. Two other offers by London and Nigerian firms asked between $2,000 and $4,000 per day. See Reuters, "British Ex-Minister to Defend Leone Rebel Leader," November 9, 1998.

19. *Sierra Leone News*, October 23, 1998, http://sierra-leone.org/slnews.html.

20. Confidential interview, June 1999.

21. BBC World Service, "Obasanjo Under Pressure over Sierra Leone," July 8, 1999.

22. U.S. Department of State, Bureau of Democracy, Human Rights, and Labor, *1999 Country Reports on Human Rights Practices: Togo*, February 25, 2000, available at http://www.state.gov/www/global/human_rights/1999_hrp_report/togo.html.

23. Interview with President Ahmad Tejan Kabbah, Freetown, June 29, 1999.

24. Interview with Dr. Vendley of the World Conference for Religion and Peace, August 1999.

25. Confidential interview, July 1999.

26. Ibid.

27. Reuters, "Sierra Leone Rebel Fighters Raise Peace Talks Stakes," July 5, 1999.

28. These included the presidents of Togo, Nigeria, Liberia, and Burkina Faso, the foreign minister of Ghana, the minister of state of Côte d'Ivoire, and representatives from the UN, OAU, ECOWAS, and the Commonwealth.

29. United Nations, *Seventh Report of the Secretary-General on the United Nations Observer Mission in Sierra Leone,* July 30, 1999, S/1999/836 contains the comment by Secretary-General Annan as well as a summary of the agreement. The Lomé Peace Agreement can be found in Appendix 2. It can also be found as United Nations, Agreement signed at Lomé, July 7, 1999, S/1999/777.

30. Lomé Peace Agreement, Article 5, Section 2, July 7, 1999, S/1999/777.

31. Lomé Peace Agreement, Article IX, Sections 1–3, July 7, 1999, S/1999/777.

32. UN spokesperson Manuel De Almeida de Silva left the UN a loophole stating, "While any sovereign state may grant amnesty for violation of its national laws . . . the United Nations will not recognize that amnesty as applying to gross violations of human rights." Cited in Nicole Winfield, "UN Won't Uphold Sierra Leone Amnesty," Associated Press, July 7, 1999. High Commissioner for Human Rights Mary Robinson welcomed the peace accord but called for an international inquiry into atrocities committed during the eight-year conflict. Sierra Leone News, "UN Rights Boss Urges Probe of Sierra Leone Abuses," July 10, 1999.

33. United Nations Security Council, *Seventh Report of the Secretary-General on the United Nations Observer Mission in Sierra Leone*, S/1999/836, July 30, 1999.

34. Lomé Peace Agreement, Article XXVI, Section 1, July 7, 1999, S/1999/777.

35. In a meeting with local NGOs in Lomé on June 22, the RUF denied that it had committed atrocities against the civilian population, charging that these were the responsibility of ECOMOG and the CDF. Interview with Zainab Bangura, Campaign for Good Governance, June 29, 1999. Sankoh was quoted at Lomé as saying, "We, the RUF, deplore all atrocities. We are asking for forgiveness for all those who have committed these atrocities, be it RUF, Kamajors, ECOMOG, or Sierra Leone Army. As a leader of a political organization I say we are sorry. We are ready to give peace a chance." Reuters, "Atrocities Cast Shadow Over Sierra Leone Accord," July 7, 1999.

36. Idrissa Conteh, "Britain Supports Peace Accord," *Concord Times* (Freetown), July 8, 1999. Susan E. Rice, assistant secretary of state for African affairs, and Gayle Smith, National Security Council senior director for African affairs, explained U.S. support for the Lomé agreement in their "Briefing on Africa," Washington, D.C., July 15, 1999, the text of which is available at http://www.un.int/usa/afrsier.htm.

37. Sankoh and Koroma met for the first time in Monrovia on October 1, and returned to Freetown on October 3. A photograph of the two fighters and President Kabbah at Lungi Airport was intended to symbolize a new spirit of cooperation.

38. United Nations Security Council, *Second Report of the Secretary-General Pursuant to Security Council Resolution 1270 (1999) on the United Nations Mission in Sierra Leone*, S/2000/13, January 11, 2000, gives the figure of disarmed within the centers as 6,000. On December 16, one day after the formal disarmament deadline, Dr. Francis Kaikai, acting executive director of the National Commission for Disarmament, Demobilization, and Reintegration (NCDDR), told the BBC that 10,557 combatants had disarmed by the deadline. He blamed logistical restraints and the mistrust among factions. (As cited in Sierra Leone News web page, December 16, 1999, http://www.sierra-leone.org.)

39. See Sierra Leone News, December 22, 1999, http://www.sierra-leone.org.

40. Senator Judd Gregg (R–New Hampshire) blocked $368 million owed by the United States to support UN peacekeeping operations in Sierra Leone, Kosovo, East Timor, and the Democratic Republic of Congo in opposition to the administration's decision to back the July 1999 plan. Reuters, "Jackson Urges U.S. Congress to Free S. Leone Funds," May 22, 2000.

41. United Nations Security Council, Resolution 1270, S/RES/1270, October 22, 1999.

42. Ibid.

43. United Nations Security Council, Resolution 1289, S/RES/1289, February 7, 2000.

44. United Nations Security Council, *Third Report of the Secretary-General on the United Nations Mission in Sierra Leone*, S/2000/186, March 7, 2000.

45. Chris McGreal, Michael Ellison, and Richard Norton-Taylor, "UN Fears Soldiers Murdered by Rebels," *The Guardian*, May 23, 2000.

46. For a summary of events in May 2000, see United Nations Security Council, *Fourth Report of the Secretary-General on the United Nations Mission in Sierra Leone*, S/2000/455, May 19, 2000.

47. Douglas Farah, "Rebel Leader Exploited U.N. Weaknesses, Officials Say," *Washington Post*, May 15, 2000.

48. Michael Ignatieff, "A Bungling UN Undermines Itself," *New York Times*, May 15, 2000; William Reno, "When Peace Is Worse Than War," *New York Times*, May 11, 2000.

49. Ralph Peters, "Sierra Leone's Blood Is on America's Hands," *Wall Street Journal*, May 11, 2000.

50. Boutros Boutros-Ghali, Supplement to an *Agenda for Peace*, United Nations, A/50/60-S/1995/1, January 3, 1995.

51. Barbara Crossette, "Sierra Leone Rebel Leader Reportedly Smuggled Gems," *New York Times*, May 14, 2000.

52. Government of Sierra Leone, "Letter from President Kabbah to Secretary-General Kofi Annan," June 12, 2000.

53. Krijn Peters and Paul Richards, "'When They Say Soldiers Are Rebels, It's a Lie': Young Fighters Talk About War and Peace in Sierra Leone," paper presented at a conference on State, Conflict, and Intervention in Sierra Leone at St. Antony's College, Oxford, May 13–14, 2000.

5

Assessment and Prospects

The Sierra Leone conflict, with its mix of external and internal forces operating on each other, can be seen as a microcosm of Africa's history in the last decade. Understanding the reasons for the country's protracted collapse and the factors underlying the limited and delayed international response to the crisis is important for prevention of similar catastrophes elsewhere in Africa. Sierra Leone was a peaceful and reasonably prosperous country at the time of independence. It now ranks at the bottom of the United Nations index for human development.[1] For the larger international community, its fate, until recently, has been inconsequential, as reflected in the disparity between responses to the crises in Kosovo and in Sierra Leone. The United Nations' consolidated humanitarian appeal for Kosovo in July 1999 was $690 million, of which 58 percent was promptly met in addition to $2.1 billion pledged for regional reconstruction. In contrast, the UN's appeal for $25 million for Sierra Leone following the conclusion of the Lomé Peace Agreement the same month was only 32 percent covered.[2] In addition to the glaring double standard between these responses, such parsimony creates an enormous obstacle to sustainable peace. By failing to provide the resources essential for disarmament and demobilization, the international community thwarts the very process to which it has pledged political support.[3]

[handwritten margin note: excessive or unusual marking by economy of sparing expenditures of money]

Financial resources, important as they are, however, are not by themselves the answer to the Sierra Leone crisis. Unless domestic and external players directly involved in the conflict reverse their pattern of winner-take-all politics and commit themselves to the national interest, the future of Sierra Leone and the surrounding region will be dire indeed. *[handwritten: desperate]* The decade-long Sierra Leone crisis has already driven hundreds of thousands of refugees into Guinea and Liberia, creating major economic and social problems and environmental degradation. Collapse of the Lomé Peace Agreement entails further destabilization for the entire region and beyond.

The challenge for the regional and international actors is to sustain political and military pressure on the Revolutionary United Front (RUF) and its external supporters while at the same time providing the wherewithal for the UN Mission in Sierra Leone (UNAMSIL) to maintain and extend its area of control into the diamond fields. The evolution of Sierra Leone's future is relevant to the ongoing search for more effective responses to Africa's post–Cold War experience of military coups and internal rebellions.

In drawing together the strands of the four preceding chapters, several stark observations need to be highlighted.

• The failure of governance over more than three decades is at the root of the Sierra Leone crisis. The corruption of government institutions, collapse of public ethics, and the failure of the education system long preceded the outbreak of the civil and cross-border war.

• The Revolutionary United Front and its external supporters, while not the only perpetrators of violence, must be held accountable for the greater part of the atrocities inflicted on the civilian population.

• The involvement of Executive Outcomes and other private security organizations must be understood as a symptom of the security vacuum before the intercessions of the Economic Community of West African States (ECOWAS) and the United Nations.

• The lucrative diamond trade contributed significantly to protracting the conflict and will continue to do so until there are effective international sanctions on illegal exports and concerted regional and international action against violators.

For most of the past decade Sierra Leone was, in William Shawcross's memorable phrase, the "Sideshow"—the offshoot of the factional war in Liberia.[4] Moreover, the crisis peaked in the aftermath of international failures to prevent the dominance of warlords in Somalia and genocide in Rwanda. The Western democracies were withdrawing from efforts to resolve Africa's internal conflicts just as the democratic government of Sierra Leone was most in need of their support. This goes far to explain the severe limitations of the international response as the crisis deepened, and the reliance on ECOWAS and its military arm, the Economic Community of West African States Cease-Fire Monitoring Group (ECOMOG), to take the lead in restoring the Kabbah government. Only late in the day did international attention, spurred on by media coverage of atrocities perpetrated in Freetown in January 1999, turn to Sierra Leone. Following strong confrontations with a defiant RUF, the international community is now asked to contribute significant resources to strengthen the presence of United Nations peacekeeping forces, as well as for the government's disarmament, demobilization, and reintegration program. If these resources are not to be wasted, the key regional and multilateral actors will have to take a resolute and united stand toward both the RUF and its principal supporter, Charles Taylor, or the crisis will only worsen. UN Secretary-General Annan, the Security Council, and the ECOWAS leadership need to maintain a rigorous high-level focus on regional as well as internal sources of subversion. At the end of this chapter I offer several recommendations as to what can be done to save Sierra Leone's battered democracy, even at this late date. Finally, I consider what broader lessons the bitter experience of Sierra Leone may have for preventing similar collapse and near anarchic conditions from occurring again elsewhere in Africa.

ASSESSMENT OF THE INTERNATIONAL RESPONSE

(worsened)

Sierra Leone's misfortunes were exacerbated by an adverse international climate militating against active measures of prevention. In the mid-1990s, against the backdrop of events in Somalia, Rwanda, and the Balkans, African and international leaders viewed the conflict with the RUF as a relatively unimportant issue in a country of marginal economic importance. As noted earlier, little or nothing was done to forestall the crisis before it began in 1991. Similarly, negotiations leading to the Abidjan Agreement in 1995–1996 garnered virtually no international attention. The "moral guarantors" of the accords (the United Nations, the Organization of African Unity (OAU), the Commonwealth, and Côte d'Ivoire) did little to follow up on its implementation in the six months before the coup. Sankoh's rejection of the proposed 750-man peacekeeping force saved the United Nations Security Council from having to make such a commitment.

International support for ECOWAS and United Nations operations following the May 1997 coup has been difficult to obtain. Overall, whatever scarce material resources were made available from the international community came only after violence erupted. Additionally, legislative restrictions barred most European Union countries from providing budgetary support for non-UN peacekeeping operations. Thus, only the United States and the United Kingdom have given direct assistance to ECOMOG, the latter after Abacha's death. It is important also to note that the concept of conflict prevention had no application in Sierra Leone. In large part, this was due to the failure to connect the Liberian and Sierra Leonean crises analytically. Additionally, while Nigeria, Ghana, and Guinea sent forces to protect the capital and its environs, only Executive Outcomes and, for a brief time, former Ghurka soldiers were actively engaged in the battle against the RUF. The competing interests of the regional states also clashed. Ghana and Côte d'Ivoire had been uncomfortable with Nigeria's dominant role in Liberia. ECOWAS's operational and financial constraints also translated into minimal attention to Sierra Leone until the crisis was full-blown.

The engagement of ECOWAS and, belatedly, the international community in a process of mediation, enforcement, and postconflict peacebuilding thus reflects the many difficulties inherent in late intervention in a crisis. The responses of the principal African and international players since May 1997 have demonstrated on the one hand the evolving willingness of a subregional organization (ECOWAS) to play a leading political and military role, and on the other its continued dependence on external support.

A separate but related issue is the role of private security forces. In the absence, until June 1997, of other international security forces, the government had no choice but to rely on Executive Outcomes. In the long run, however, private forces cannot be seen as the solution to Africa's security problems.

The following are brief commentaries on the role of major players as the crisis developed.

The Organization of African Unity

If the May 1997 coup took the international community by surprise, for the Organization of African Unity it has been an important turning point, a first move away from the principle of noninterference in the internal affairs of states enshrined in its 1963 charter. The condemnation of the coup at the Harare summit was a significant development, particularly as many African leaders had come to power themselves through coups. However, this was already late in the day. The OAU had supported a negotiated settlement of the conflict but, with its headquarters in Addis Ababa, it was too remote from the scene to follow clearly what was happening. The assignment of a mid-level official to the Abidjan and Lomé negotiations reflected the limited personnel available at OAU headquarters and the relatively low priority accorded to the conflict. The OAU's conflict-resolution mechanism was never brought to bear in a significant way in seeking to resolve the crisis.

The Economic Community of West African States

As the international community hesitated to act, ECOWAS emerged as the central actor in efforts to broker and support a durable settlement. Inevitably, Nigeria, as ECOMOG's largest troop contributor, played the key role in the military action that drove the junta out of Freetown. While Western countries severely criticized General Sani Abacha's human rights record at home, it is important to note that without ECOMOG's intervention President Kabbah would not have been able to return to Freetown in

March 1998. Many observers have found an irony in General Abacha being credited with restoring a democratically elected president. In assessing the strange relationship that developed between Kabbah and Abacha, it is clear that the latter was far less interested in the cause of democracy than in Nigeria's hegemonic position in the subregion.[5] Yet Abacha did not have a free hand to do whatever he wanted. Ghana and Côte d'Ivoire were determined to have a voice in shaping ECOWAS policy and they were strongly opposed to the military option. Thus, on top of resource constraints, internal political tensions also impacted on ECOWAS policy. Francophone/ Anglophone tensions, Ivorian and Ghanaian sensitivities to Nigeria's dominance, and ECOWAS's continued preoccupation with Liberia gave the Armed Forces Revolutionary Council (AFRC)/RUF junta a limited amount of time to maneuver. Moreover, as long as Liberia and Burkina Faso were directly or indirectly supporting the RUF, ECOWAS was unable to act in a united way.

Since Abacha's death, ECOWAS's role in Sierra Leone has changed in a number of complex ways. Under severe domestic pressure, President Obasanjo's decision to end ECOMOG's presence in Sierra Leone has placed greater responsibility on the United Nations force. Even as Nigerian troops have become subsumed into UNAMSIL battalions, it is clear that Nigeria continues to play a major military and political role.

As negotiators, ECOWAS representatives have had varying effectiveness. Ivorian foreign minister Amara Essy played a pivotal albeit controversial role in the Abidjan process, patiently putting up with RUF demands for almost a year. He pressed Kabbah to give Sankoh the vice presidency; whether this would have solidified the agreement remains an open issue. After the coup, Nigerian foreign minister Ikimi took the key role in directing the ECOWAS Committee of Four (and then Five). Notwithstanding his abrasive and imperious personality, the committee maintained political pressure on the junta and obtained UN Security Council support for ECOWAS's sanctions. While several Security Council members had reservations about being asked without sufficient prior consultation to follow ECOWAS's lead, the sanctions adopted at the Abuja summit in August were given international application in UNSC Resolution 1132 of October 8, 1997. ECOWAS's military actions in liberating Freetown were also endorsed by the Security Council.

The United Nations

The United Nations has played an important role as one of the key mediators at Abidjan and Lomé and in seeking to implement the National Commission for Disarmament, Demobilization, and Reintegration (NCDDR) programs. These activities reflect its strengths in fielding high-quality special representatives and its manifold weakness in the management of complex programs. Its efforts also suffered from a conceptual mistake. The crisis in Sierra Leone was regional in nature, yet the UN designated its operations on a country level. With special envoys for Sierra Leone and Liberia, the UN, like the United States and the United Kingdom, arbitrarily compartmentalized its policy. While Dinka was a major participant in the Abidjan negotiations, the UN did not treat Sierra Leone as a regional crisis until after the May 1997 coup. However, as Africans (Dinka is Ethiopian, Okelo is Ugandan, Adeniji is Nigerian), the special representatives were well placed to understand the political and personality-driven dynamics of ECOWAS and the OAU. They persevered despite major constraints—from Sankoh's hostile attitude to the UN to the structure of the Abidjan negotiations and Ikimi's determination to maintain absolute control of talks with the AFRC/RUF.

The UN's greatest difficulty in Sierra Leone, however, has been lack of interagency coordination and poor interaction with the large and diverse international NGO community. The fact that President Kabbah came himself from a UN background made it harder for him to make the necessary decisions to improve coordination. This had the greatest impact on the UN's inability to launch the disarmament and demilitarization program in late 1996/early 1997. The National Reconstruction, Rehabilitation and Resettlement Ministry, responsible for administering this program, was riddled with inefficiency and corruption. The UN Resident Representative sought as a remedy to increase the ministry's staff with qualified expatriates. Nine months were lost until President Kabbah transferred the program over to the State House.

There were also various misconceived attempts to control the independently minded NGOs, which inevitably backfired. A major problem arose while the Kabbah government was in exile in Conakry. In response to the UN Security Council–mandated embargo, Okelo joined Kabbah and the Guinean government in seeking to ensure that humanitarian relief supplies did not assist the junta. Acrimonious discussions exacerbated Okelo's relationship with the NGOs, who interpreted their responsibility as nonpolitical deliverers of humanitarian assistance. United Nations efforts to integrate its relief and development programs within a "strategic framework" will encounter similar difficulties unless implementation is handled in a noncoercive and sensitive manner.

Multilateral Organizations

The International Monetary Fund's (IMF) structural adjustment programs, as well as World Bank and European Union (EU) programs in support of disarmament, demobilization, and reconstruction, have suffered from lack of effective coordination with the United Nations. Institutional rivalries, delays in assigning key IMF and EU staff to Freetown, and the absence of a resident World Bank office severely constrained their effectiveness. In the narrow time frame from the 1996 election to the coup, governance programs inevitably had little impact. While the IMF provided balance-of-payments support, and World Bank teams sought to create a programmatic basis for development, their complex regulations and closed-door procedures meant that planning lacked transparency and resonance. Representatives of civil society were excluded from their negotiations with government. The EU's role was hampered by overregulation from Brussels. Only a small amount of the estimated $1 billion available in the 1995–1999 time frame under the Lomé convention was disbursed.

The United Kingdom

As the former colonial power, the United Kingdom has taken the leading non-African role in seeking a long-term resolution to the crisis. Tony Blair's decision to mount a major military intervention in May 2000 served the dual purpose of stabilizing the security situation in and around Freetown, and bolstering UNAMSIL's capacity at a critical moment of confrontation with the RUF. In the longer term, its role will remain important but constrained by domestic political considerations. From 1986 to 1997, when Baroness Linda Chalker led African policy in the Foreign Office, the British supported the National Provisional Ruling Council's efforts to put down the rebellion; then provided significant political and financial support for the 1996 election; and subsequently worked actively for the ouster of the AFRC/RUF junta and Kabbah's restoration. British policy during the junta's control of Freetown focused on enlarging the sanctions initially adopted by ECOWAS, which were given international application in UN Security Council Resolution 1132 (October 1997). British policy, however, precluded financial or military support to ECOMOG as long as Abacha remained at the helm in Nigeria. (position of leadership or control)

[handwritten margin note: prevented]

The Sandline affair created a major embarrassment for Foreign Secretary Robin Cook.[6] As recounted in Chapter 4, press accounts suggested that British officials had knowingly violated the United Nations embargo on arms to Sierra Leone that Cook's chief legal adviser had drafted. British officials allegedly had introduced Sandline to Kabbah, opening the way for the contractual arrangement whereby Sandline would provide arms and logistical support to ECOMOG. A photograph in the *Sunday Times* showed a Sandline helicopter being maintained abroad the frigate *HMS Cornwall* in Freetown harbor.[7] There were conflicting legal interpretations

of whether the embargo applied to both the rebels and the Kabbah government, since its objective was the latter's restoration, but this did not stop
hostile editorialists from attacks on Cook's "ethical foreign policy." A parliamentary inquiry (the Legg Report) ultimately characterized the incident
as a function of incompetence (different departments not being coordinated
with each other), but the alleged involvement of British intelligence was
played down.

Even before the May 2000 crisis, Britain extended financial support to
ECOMOG, and it remains the primary bilateral donor to Sierra Leone, providing training for the police and a new army. Britain has been less successful in persuading its partners in the European Union to make any substantial commitments.

The United States

Through most of the 1990s, U.S. policy in West Africa was focused on ending the conflict in Liberia. This included support for ECOMOG operations
and a major role in negotiating the framework for the July 1997 elections in
that country. Sierra Leone remained of relatively low priority to overall
U.S. foreign policy interests in Africa, as it was viewed as primarily
Britain's responsibility. U.S. policy slowly evolved to an acceptance of the
need for a broader framework, including Sierra Leone, for regional security. Following the May 1997 coup, Washington accepted the concept of a
security nexus between Sierra Leone and Liberia, and placed considerable
diplomatic pressure on Taylor to cease his support for the RUF as a condition for continued U.S. economic assistance. U.S. support for ECOMOG
and UNAMSIL operations in Sierra Leone, Jesse Jackson's personal diplomacy in brokering the April 1999 cease-fire, and close cooperation with the
British in support of the Lomé Peace Agreement represented a significant
and positive shift. The October 22, 1999, visit of Secretary of State
Madeleine Albright to Freetown followed by the visit of Congressmen
Tony P. Hall (Ohio) and Frank R. Wolf (Virginia) on December 6–7, 1999,
were reflections of new U.S. concern.[8] In voting for progressive expansion
of UNAMSIL, the United States has committed itself to paying a quarter of
its operating costs, which, according to UN official estimates, is approaching $782.2 million.[9] Additionally, President Clinton authorized the
Pentagon to spend up to $20 million to support the mission. Most of this
money was allocated for training of Nigerian peacekeeping units as well as
the U.S. airlift of Indian and Jordanian forces. In response to the events in
May, upon British insistence and with considerable pressure from
Ambassador Richard Holbrooke in New York, the United States and the
UK developed three key Security Council initiatives: the diamond embar-
go, an international tribunal, and the effort to strengthen UNAMSIL.[10]

Other Donors

A brief word will suffice in regard to other donors. Most countries have followed events through their representatives at the United Nations, but their interest and involvement have been very limited. France closed its embassy in December 1996 for budgetary reasons (along with its embassies in Liberia, Jamaica, and Malawi). Germany reduced its level of representation after the National Provisional Ruling Council ousted Ambassador Karl Prinz in early 1995 for meeting with Charles Taylor, and closed its embassy in February 2000, also for budgetary reasons. Other non-African countries have followed Sierra Leone only intermittently from their embassies elsewhere in West Africa. Notwithstanding continued discussions in the Security Council, few potential donor countries are well informed.

SIERRA LEONE AT THE CROSSROADS

In the aftermath of these events, any prognosis for Sierra Leone's future can only be provisional. After almost a decade of war and three flawed agreements, Sierra Leone remains in a precarious situation. The international community, having made an increased commitment since 1997, must now decide whether it is prepared to take the hard steps necessary to end the conflict. In the short term, the country's most pressing need is security. Three aspects are essential: (1) strengthening of UNAMSIL's command structure and resource base; (2) military and political pressure to deny the RUF and its external supporters continued access to the diamond fields; and (3) an effective disarmament process as the precondition for the next elections. The RUF rank and file should continue to be encouraged to disarm voluntarily but also be made to understand that the RUF will not be allowed to take power by force.

I propose the following four challenges for the international community:

1. *Revising the post-Lomé strategy:* The United Nations and ECOWAS can no longer base their strategy on the flawed assumption of dealing with a more or less rational organization committed to peace. The RUF's failure to meet its obligations under the Lomé Peace Agreement has undermined its residual credibility as an interlocutor in the peace process. The political provisions of the agreement should be held in abeyance, including funding for its transformation into a political party, participation in the Cabinet, and chairmanship of the Commission for the Management of Strategic Resources (which was a bad idea in the first place). The regional and international signatories must sustain political as well as mili-

[handwritten margin note: dangerously lacking in security & stability]

tary pressure on the RUF leadership to lay down their weapons and relinquish control of the diamond fields. The arms embargo and travel ban, including on RUF family members, should remain in force until the disarmament provisions of the peace agreement are fulfilled. The pattern of concessions and appeasement of the RUF needs to be replaced by a forceful and unequivocal stance.

2. *Prosecuting war criminals:* The blanket amnesty granted to the RUF under the Lomé Peace Agreement does not apply to crimes committed since July 7, 1999. The Security Council's decision to create an international tribunal to prosecute those who have committed crimes against humanity and violations of international humanitarian law constitutes a major step forward. The tribunal will have to decide which other groups or individuals, apart from Foday Sankoh and the senior RUF leadership, who have also committed acts of violence against United Nations peacekeepers and Sierra Leoneans in this timeframe fall under its jurisdiction. This is a complex political as well as legal issue that needs to be addressed scrupulously. The amnesty should remain in effect only for those rank and file who participate in the disarmament process. Additionally, it is essential that the tribunal be established on the basis of assessed, not voluntary, contributions by United Nations member states in order to have both viability and legitimacy. It is incumbent on Secretary-General Annan to press the Security Council to revise its enabling mandate accordingly.[11]

3. *Dealing with Liberia:* The key to determining the RUF's future, now that Sankoh is to be prosecuted, lies more clearly than ever with Charles Taylor. His effective intervention with the RUF and continued involvement with diamond mining and marketing underscore the centrality and complexity of his role. In effect, Taylor has been both mediator and spoiler. The Secretary-General's May 15, 2000, report praises Taylor's role in obtaining the release of the UN peacekeepers. Taylor, however, has long had his own agenda for Sierra Leone. For now the arms embargo on Liberia should be kept in place and the ban on Sierra Leone's conflict diamonds instituted. The United States in particular needs to press Taylor to end his support for the RUF. Otherwise, he should face suspension of bilateral assistance as well as other international sanctions including freezing of personal and official assets. Similar sanctions should be applied to Burkina Faso if the evidence indicates its continued support for the RUF.

4. *Strengthening West African security capacity:* While the immediate focus of the international community is on strengthening UNAMSIL, the political and military leaders of ECOWAS have been actively engaged over the past two years in developing the foundation for a permanent security force for the West African subregion. At the Lomé ECOWAS summit of

December 1999, heads of state agreed to establish a conflict resolution mechanism to deal with embryonic and ongoing conflicts. The goal is to facilitate prompt regional political and military action to deal with military coups and external interventions. With a democratically elected civilian government in place in Nigeria, the international community should support this new initiative with logistical and financial resources. This course of action is far preferable to having vulnerable regimes rely on private security forces such as Executive Outcomes to assist them.[12]

Over and above these immediate issues, peace and stability will require the transformation of Sierra Leone's political culture. The country's political elites need to change their attitudes, placing a commitment to the nation above self-aggrandizement and personal enrichment. Democratic values, the rule of law, and human rights have to be honored in practice, not just in the abstract. The Kabbah government must be helped to assure openness and accountability, especially in the minerals sector. The politics of intimidation and violence, which characterized Sierra Leone's postindependence history, needs to be replaced by a culture of tolerance and mutual respect. A first step must be acknowledgment by the RUF of its violent deeds. The Truth and Reconciliation Commission can only be meaningful if the perpetrators of the violence are made to take responsibility for their actions. At the same time, revitalization of civil society needs to take place in order to develop public oversight and effective interaction with the government and external donors. Short-term programs that would allow qualified Sierra Leoneans residing abroad to provide their skills in rebuilding the nation need to be developed and funded.

At some distance, the Sierra Leone crisis would seem to reinforce Robert Kaplan's dire and sweeping predictions in "The Coming Anarchy."[13] Viewed under a more scrupulous lens, the Sierra Leone case would appear less clear-cut. The political and economic processes in the country are in the midst of a long-term transition, the ultimate outcome of which remains to be seen. In the short term, there is a strong regional and international commitment to support the peace process. On the other hand, those who derive profit from conflict remain in place. The role of the RUF's external supporters remains ambiguous. A country cannot somehow be saved, as a man who has fallen overboard from an ocean liner, by a single life buoy. In the current international climate, it would be foolhardy to predict whether the requisite financial and human resources can be found and sustained over the medium to long term (one to ten years). Those directly involved need to understand that this is probably the last chance to save what is left to save. The next presidential and parliamentary elections are due to take place in the first half of 2001. Elections by themselves, however, are no assurance of either stability or development.

A major theme of this chapter has been the importance of reviving the democratic political process at the national and regional level. It has to be acknowledged that civil society, which promoted the 1996 election, has suffered a significant setback. Many civil-society leaders and advocates were forced to flee when the AFRC/RUF took over in Freetown. The cohesion and impact of civil society has been drastically weakened since then. The Campaign for Good Governance, the Inter-Religious Council, and others remain active, yet it will require considerably improved security and stability to persuade even a few of those who have left the country to come back. Civil society, especially the religious community, can play a major role in encouraging the revival of local conflict-resolution mechanisms in the rural areas. Traditional rituals perhaps can provide a catharsis for those who have been traumatized by the fighting and atrocities of the past decade.

Ultimately, Sierra Leone's future depends on the quality and values of its leadership. South Africa avoided calamity through the leadership of Nelson Mandela and F. W. De Klerk, who understood that compromise was better than bloodshed, and placed the national interest in peace and reconciliation above partisan aspirations. In Sierra Leone there may still be that opportunity. Public resilience is extraordinary, and the capacity for forgiveness great. At a civil-society conference in Senegal in December 1999, a Burundian civil-society leader quoted a local proverb: "Ipito gitabwa iwabo." An approximate translation would be that "even the worst person in society must ultimately return to his community." It seems appropriate to the current situation in Sierra Leone. One can only hope that this latest and perhaps last opportunity for peace and reconciliation—however painful it is to grasp—will yet be seized.

The tragedy of Sierra Leone, as I have argued throughout this volume, is that it falls below the threshold of major-power strategic significance. Nonetheless, even at this late date, a resolute international force, united regional diplomacy, and reconciliation with those in the RUF rank and file who truly want peace can avert further catastrophe. As to the broader significance of this story, the international community—and especially the major powers—must move to a higher level of early preventive action and sustained engagement in intrastate and regional conflicts. Secretary-General Annan, in his address to the Fifty-fourth General Assembly, called for the international community to embrace a "common interest" above the narrowly defined national agendas that ignore such evolving tragedies until they engulf all of us. From both a moral and rational perspective, there is urgent need for a heightened international awareness of our collective responsibility to the forces of democracy alive today in Africa and the generations yet to come.

NOTES

1. See the Human Development Index (HDI) in United Nations Development Programme, *Human Development Report 1999: Globalization with a Human Face,* New York, July 12, 1999. Sierra Leone is last on the list at number 174.

2. Victoria Brittain, "Unrealistic Humanitarians," *The Guardian* (London), August 4, 1999.

3. See Kofi A. Annan, "Africa: The Horror and the Hope," *Washington Post,* August 1, 1999.

4. William Shawcross, *Deliver Us from Evil: Peacekeepers, Warlords, and a World of Endless Conflict* (New York: Simon and Schuster, 2000), pp. 118–145.

5. Adekeye Adebajo, "West Africa's Tragic Twins: Building Peace in Liberia and Sierra Leone," paper presented at the Symposium on Peacebuilding in Post-Conflict Societies, University of Alberta, Edmonton, March 10, 2000, p. 5.

6. See Ian Douglas, "Fighting for Diamonds: Private Military Companies in Sierra Leone," in Jakkie Cilliers and Peggy Mason (eds.), *Peace, Profit, or Plunder? The Privatisation of Security in War-Torn African Societies* (Johannesburg, South Africa: Institute for Security Studies, Halfway House, 1999), pp. 186–195 for a detailed account of the complex relationship between Sandline, Kabbah, and the British government during the period of Kabbah's exile.

7. Nicholas Rufford, "First Proof of Navy Role in Coup," *Sunday Times,* May 10, 1998, p. 1.

8. Representative Frank Wolf, focusing on the role of diamonds, was quoted as saying, "The world looked the other way in Angola for most of the 1990s, while revenues from diamond sales were used to butcher innocent civilians. We should not stand by as the same thing happens in Sierra Leone . . . We should do whatever it takes to cut off the flow of money." In Blaine Harden, "Africa's Gems: Warfare's Best Friend," *New York Times,* April 6, 2000, p. A1.

For further details on Congress's Commitment to Sierra Leone, see U.S. Congress, Sierra Leone Peace Support Act of 2000, H.R. 3879, introduced in the House of Representatives on March 9, 2000.

9. As cited in United Nations Security Council, *Sixth Report of the Secretary-General on the United Nations Mission in Sierra Leone,* Addendum, September 12, 2000, S/2000/832/Add.1, with an increased strength of 20,500 personnel, UNAMSILS costs should grow to $782.2 million for the year beginning July 2000. This would mean the United States is slotted to pay up to $200 million.

10. See United Nations Security Council, Resolution 1306 on the situation in Sierra Leone, July 5, 2000, S/2000/1306 on the diamond embargo; UN Security Council, Resolution 1315, August 14, 2000, S/2000/1315 on the international tribunal; and United Nations, Security Council, *Sixth Report of the Secretary-General on the United Nations Mission in Sierra Leone,* August 24, 2000, S/2000/832 for the request to increase troop strength.

11. The Secretary General has recommended to the Security Council that (1) the temporal jurisdiction of the Special Court should start on November 30, 1996, the date of the Abidjan Peace Agreement; (2) its jurisdiction should extend to the persons most responsible for the commission of the proscribed crimes; and (3) a Juvenile Chamber be established to consider prosecution of children between the ages of 15 and 18 for crimes against humanity and war crimes. *Report of the Secretary-General on the Establishment of a Special Court for Sierra Leone,* United Nations Security Council, S/2000/915, October 4, 2000.

12. See Eric G. Berman and Katie E. Sams, *Peacekeeping in Africa:*

Capabilities and Culpabilities, United Nations Institute for Disarmament Research (UNIDIR), Geneva, Switzerland, UNIDIR/2000/3, pp. 138–145, for an account of the evolution and structure of the draft "ECOWAS Mechanism for Conflict Prevention, Management and Resolution Peacekeeping and Security," subsequently adopted by ECOWAS heads of state in Lomé, December 1999.

13. Robert Kaplan, "The Coming Anarchy," *Atlantic Monthly,* February 1994.

Postscript,
September 1, 2000

Since these chapters were completed, the international community has taken a number of steps toward a more robust effort to resolve the Sierra Leone crisis. Most notably the Security Council has decided to establish an embargo on conflict diamonds, agreed to set up an international tribunal to prosecute those responsible for the most grievous human rights violations, and moved to further enlarge UNAMSIL's troop strength.[1] There is increased international and regional pressure on President Taylor to desist from extending support to the RUF or selling conflict diamonds (charges which he denies), including European Union suspension of loans and reduced United States economic assistance. Presidents Obasanjo and Konare have reportedly delivered stern messages to Taylor regarding his obligation to honor ECOWAS support for the Lomé Peace Agreement. United States Special Forces have initiated a training program for Nigerian army units assigned to UNAMSIL to include a focus on human rights and international humanitarian law.

These are positive developments. But they must be regarded at best as incremental steps in a long process. The challenge of ending Sierra Leone's protracted agony and beginning its reconstruction remain. With Foday Sankoh again in Pademba Road Prison, along with a number of his senior associates, the RUF has named Field Commander Issa Sesay as a new "interim leader." It has undertaken to return equipment seized from UNAMSIL forces over past months. However, these steps do not change the fundamental reality that Sierra Leone is still in a war situation, divided between areas under government and UNAMSIL control and areas including the diamond fields still held by the RUF. The rebels, by their violation of preceding peace agreements and continued military activity, have destroyed whatever residual credibility they may have retained as an interlocutor in the peace process. The challenge for the United Nations is not to negotiate further cease-fires and amnesties but to press aggressively for the

RUF to lay down its arms. This will require that UNAMSIL take control of the diamond region, if necessary by force, and that political pressure on the Liberian and Burkinabe governments—including, if necessary, the application of sanctions—be sustained. Decisions on the timing of the next election and assistance to the RUF to become a political party should be left in abeyance until the military situation is redressed in UNAMSIL's favor.

On August 23 the United Nations released the findings of an independent panel, chaired by former Algerian Foreign Minister Lakhdar Brahimi, on measures needed to strengthen United Nations peace operations.[2] The report is notable for its candor in highlighting the failures of past and ongoing operations, including in Sierra Leone. The report urges the Secretary-General to tell the Security Council what it needs to hear, not what it wants to hear. United Nations forces need to be given both the mandate and the means to fight, particularly where the conflict is not resolved by the signing of a peace agreement. It calls for the Secretary-General and the Security Council to distinguish clearly between aggressors and victims, in place of the much abused concept of impartiality that "in the worst [case] may amount to complicity with evil." The report also urges the Secretary-General to take a much more proactive approach to peacekeeping. This means more active involvement in promoting the rule of law and economic recovery by integrating military and police operations with reconstruction and civil administration functions, especially in states and regions where local governments have collapsed. These are all useful recommendations that merit the support of the permanent members of the Security Council.

Inevitably United Nations forces will remain in Sierra Leone only for a limited time. This is also the moment, therefore, as I noted at the end of Chapter 5, to strengthen ECOWAS's ongoing efforts to create a permanent standby regional force. With a democratic government in Abuja, there is a clear opportunity for the international community to support a new security architecture for West Africa.[3] At this juncture the means to bring the Sierra Leone conflict to a close, or at least to severely contain it, are at hand. It is a juncture of limited duration; an opportunity that should not be squandered. The future not only of Sierra Leone but of prospects for stability in the entire West African subregion are at stake.

NOTES

1. See United Nations Security Council Resolution 1306 on the situation in Sierra Leone, July 5, 2000; S/2000/1306 on the embargo of diamonds; UN Security Council Resolution 1313, August 4, 2000, S/2000/1313 on the changing military

mandate; UN Security Council Resolution 1315, August 14, 2000, S/2000/1315 on the setting up of an international tribunal; and United Nations, *Sixth Report of the Secretary-General on the United Nations Mission in Sierra Leone*, August 24, 2000, S/2000/832 and S/2000/ 832/Add.1 for a discussion of increasing mission strength to 20,500.

2. Report of the Panel on United Nations Peace Operations, A/55/305-S/2000/809, August 21, 2000.

3. See Adekeye Adebajo and David Keen, "Banquet for Warlords," *The World Today*, July 2000.

Appendix 1

Chronology:
Selected Events in Sierra Leone

1462	Portuguese explorer Pedro da Cintra maps the hills overlooking Freetown harbor, calling the formation Serra Lyoa (Lion Range).
c. 1750	Bunce Island becomes a major West African slave port under British control.
1787	Four hundred freed slaves settle in Freetown.
1807	British Parliament votes to prohibit the Atlantic slave trade.
1808	Freetown is made a British Crown Colony.
1833	British Parliament makes slavery illegal.
1896	Governor Cardew declares a protectorate over the region, including areas occupied by the interior tribes.
1898	The Hut Tax War begins at Port Loko as the result of Governor Cardew's tax of 25 pence on each household.
1914	Railroad construction is completed, linking coastal and interior regions with railways to the diamond mines.
1947	The British introduce proposals linking the Crown Colony and the protectorate.
1953	The British establish a new bureaucratic system, leading to wider diffusion of political power to local chiefs.
1961	Independence is declared on April 27. Sir Milton Margai, a prominent physician, is elected prime minister, head of the Sierra Leone People's Party (SLPP).

1964		Prime Minister Milton Margai dies and is succeeded by his brother, Sir Albert Margai.
1964		Sir Albert Margai attempts to amend the constitution to create a one-party state, but the initiative fails.
1967		All People's Congress (APC) leader Siaka Stevens wins elections with support of northerners and Krios. A coup led by Brigadier David Lansana prevents him from taking office. Senior officers, organized as the National Reformation Council (NRC), arrest Lansana and suspend the national constitution.
1968		Noncommissioned officers stage Sierra Leone's third coup in thirteen months. Siaka Stevens returns to power and restores the constitution.
1970		A state of emergency is declared due to provincial disturbances.
1971		A new republican constitution is adopted.
1978		Stevens adopts a single-party constitution.
1985		Major General Joseph Momoh, Stevens's military force commander, is handpicked to succeed Stevens as president.
1990		Momoh supports return to multiparty democracy and oversees writing of new constitution. Elections are scheduled for 1992.
1991	March 23	Around 100 fighters, including Sierra Leonean dissidents, Liberian fighters loyal to Charles Taylor, and a small number of mercenaries from Burkina Faso, invade eastern Sierra Leone. The Revolutionary United Front (RUF), led by Corporal Foday Sankoh, takes responsibility.
	May	The RUF, using vague populist rhetoric, launches a war against farmers, villagers, and alluvial miners to demonstrate the inability of the Momoh government to protect its citizens. Britain turns down Momoh's request for military advisers, communications, and intelligence capacity. Over the following months, the Sierra Leone Army scrambles to recruit new troops, many of whom are young and untrained, to send to the front. Without adequate training, supplies, or logistical and medical support, they are unable to effectively defend the territory.
	August	Sierra Leoneans vote overwhelmingly in a referen-

		dum to introduce a multiparty system. The 1991 Multiparty Constitution is endorsed and passed into law.
1992	January	Rebel operations in the diamond-rich areas in the southeast indicate a new strategy of attacking strategic economic targets.
	April 29	Junior officers carry out a bloodless coup. Momoh flees to Guinea. The officers form the National Provisional Ruling Council (NPRC), selecting Captain Valentine Strasser as chairman.
	November	The NPRC launches a major offensive against the RUF, dislodging the rebels from the diamond-rich southeast. For some months the rebels are pushed into Liberia, where they allegedly receive extensive support from National Patriotic Front of Liberia (NPFL) faction leader Charles Taylor.
1993	March	The rebels regroup and intensify their attacks on rural villages, creating a growing number of civilian casualties. Two battalions of Nigerian troops are moved from Monrovia to Freetown to assist Strasser. Nigerian Alpha jets are based in Freetown for bombing raids against Taylor's NPFL.
	December	Civil service salaries fall to an average of $18 per month, schools operate sporadically, and certain ministries are unreachable as their phones have been disconnected.
1994	January	The NPRC launches an army recruitment drive, signing up poorly educated youth and orphans from the age of twelve upwards. Army ranks increase to 12,000. New soldiers loot and pillage the towns and villages up-country until many refer to them as *sobels*, soldier-rebels who are soldiers during the day and rebels at night.
	September	Nigeria and Sierra Leone enter into a Mutual Defense Pact.
1995	January 6	Strasser offers the RUF a six-point peace plan, threatening increased military action should the plan be refused.
	January 10	A delegation of civil society representatives arrives in Liberia for discussions with RUF representatives.
	January 18–19	The RUF overruns the Sierra Rutile and Sieromco Mines, severely damaging the government's rev-

	enue base in the midst of a tough structural-adjustment program.
January 26	The NPRC issues a mobilization order for police and soldiers to fight against the RUF forces, who are within forty kilometers of Freetown.
February 1	The NPRC asks the International Committee of the Red Cross (ICRC) to arrange a meeting with the RUF.
February	RUF fighters advance toward the capital. The NPRC relies heavily on the 2,000 Nigerians based in Freetown. The Ghurkha security guards retreat after their leader, U.S. Colonel Robert Mackenzie, is killed. The UN appoints Berhanu Dinka as special envoy to negotiate a settlement of the conflict.
March	Strasser enters into a contract with Executive Outcomes (EO), a South African private security force, to provide security assistance. Run by Eeben Barlow, formerly of the South African Defense Forces, EO members had been active in covert operations in Mozambique and Angola. EO starts training programs for the Sierra Leone Army.
March 19	The army, with close air support provided by Executive Outcomes, retakes Moyamba.
April 27	Strasser lifts the ban on political parties and offers amnesty to the RUF.
May	EO joins Nigerian and Ghanaian troops in defending Freetown, driving the RUF back.
August 16–20	The National Consultative Conference (Bintumani I) meets, scheduling elections for February 1996.
December	EO expands operations into rural areas, taking back the diamond-mining areas. EO initiates cooperation with the (Mende-controlled) Kamajoh traditional militia, a local defense force, by providing training and logistical support.
1996 Early January	EO retakes the Sierra Rutile Mine. Kamajohs and EO fight the RUF in its rural strongholds.
January 16	Brigadier-General Julius Maada Bio replaces Strasser as NPRC chairman in a palace coup. Maada Bio promises elections will be held on schedule. Freetown's market women march through the city, threatening to expose politicians receiving bribes from the military to halt the election process.

February 16	Bio reconvenes the Bintumani conference to consider postponing elections (Bintumani II); overwhelming majority favor going ahead as scheduled.
February 26–27	Presidential and legislative elections are held with the participation of thirteen political parties. None of the presidential candidates receive the required 55 percent vote.
March 15	In a runoff round, Ahmad Tejan Kabbah of the Sierra Leone People's Party (SLPP) defeats John Karefa Smart of the United National People's Party (UNPP).
March 17	Kabbah is declared the winner with 59.9 percent of the vote. Runner-up John Karefa-Smart complains of widespread fraud. Under Kabbah, EO continues its work with the Kamajohs, who become an increasingly powerful military and political force. Hinga Norman, former Kamajoh leader, is appointed deputy minister of defense.
March 25–26	Discussions between Bio and Sankoh in Yamoussoukro, Côte d'Ivoire, end with reaffirmation of the two-month-long cease-fire and an agreement to allow delivery of humanitarian aid to areas under RUF control. Sankoh agrees to meet with the future government to continue talks.
March 29	Bio transfers power to the civilian government in a ceremony at the parliament. Kabbah is sworn in as president.
April 22	Sankoh and Kabbah start peace talks in Yamoussoukro, Côte d'Ivoire.
April 23	President Kabbah and Sankoh agree on an indefinite cease-fire. Three working groups meet May 6–28 in Abidjan where a draft peace agreement is formulated.
May 29	Negotiations on a peace agreement are suspended over the contentious issue of the withdrawal of foreign forces and Executive Outcomes.
July	Discontent in the army increases with the announcement of a plan to dramatically reduce the size of the army and reduce its rice rations, also causing uncertainty about pension benefits.
July 25	The International Monetary Fund (IMF) reports Sierra Leone's GDP shrank by 10 percent in 1995

	while inflation is reported to have increased to 35 percent per annum.
August	Nigerian and EO attacks increase pressure on RUF forces. London-based International Alert seeks to renew negotiations between the RUF and Kabbah in Côte d'Ivoire.
September	EO is charging $1.8 million a month for the services of less than 100 personnel along with two Russian helicopters and logistics. As a result of IMF requirements, pressing for government cuts in spending, Kabbah renegotiates the EO fee. Independent sources report that the government still owes $30 million in arrears from the NPRC.
September 9	A coup attempt against President Kabbah's government is detected and aborted. Major Johnny Paul Koroma is arrested.
September 13	The government orders retired soldiers to turn in their weapons.
September 16	The government approves Sankoh's request to return to Kailahun to consult his field commanders on the proposed peace agreement.
October 24	Kabbah and Sankoh meet in Abidjan with President Henri Conan Bedie of Côte d'Ivoire to again urge Sankoh's return to Sierra Leone.
November 15	The government agrees to grant a general amnesty to RUF fighters in the context of the peace agreement.
November 30	Kabbah and Sankoh sign the Abidjan Peace Agreement. The UN, Commonwealth, Organization of African Unity (OAU), and the government of Côte d'Ivoire serve as moral guarantors. EO is required, in the agreement, to leave following establishment of a neutral monitoring group. EO affiliate Lifeguard renews its security contracts with several mining companies.
December 18	Eleven people are arrested for plotting a second coup.
December 19	The Commission for the Consolidation of Peace (CCP) is formally launched in Freetown with the attendance of RUF representatives Ibrahim Deen-Jalloh and Faya Musa.
1997 January 31	EO officially departs Sierra Leone. The cabinet is reshuffled and reduced from twenty-six to eighteen

ministries. The Commission for the Consolidation of Peace is unable to develop a disarmament plan as Sankoh fails to appoint representatives to the disarmament and demobilization subcommittee, and the process falters.

February 3   The UN High Commissioner for Refugees begins repatriation of refugees located in Liberia. The last members of Executive Outcomes depart Sierra Leone.

March 6   Foday Sankoh flies secretly to Lagos, Nigeria, reportedly to purchase weapons. He is arrested in the Lagos Airport parking lot for illegal possession of weapons. At Kabbah's request, Abacha agrees to hold Sankoh in Nigeria.

March 7   Sierra Leone and Nigeria renew the 1994 Mutual Defense Agreement.

March 15   RUF commander Philip Palmer, speaking on BBC radio from Danane, Côte d'Ivoire, announces a decision of some RUF leaders to remove Sankoh from the leadership. The coup attempt fails when four coup leaders are arrested in Kailahun by field commander Sam Bockarie.

April 17   The United Kingdom and Sierra Leone sign an agreement for British military training of two battalions of the Sierra Leone Army.

May 8   The IMF allocates a $14 million loan to Sierra Leone in recognition of the progress in reaching economic targets.

May 25   A group of junior officers stages a coup. Major Johnny Paul Koroma and hundreds more are released from prison. Koroma assumes power as chairman of the Armed Forces Revolutionary Council (AFRC). President Kabbah flees to Guinea. There is extensive looting, killing, and mistreatment of civilians including members of the Kabbah government and administration. The Ministry of Finance is torched.

May 26   In a night operation, Nigerian and Guinean contingents of the Economic Community of West African States Cease-Fire Monitoring Group (ECOMOG) land at Hastings and Lungi Airports where they establish control.

May 27	The AFRC suspends Sierra Leone's constitution and bans political parties.
May 28	The RUF high command orders its fighters to support the AFRC.
May 29	AFRC soldiers assume control of the diamond mines in Koidu.
May 30	U.S. Marines evacuate 900 people from Freetown to the *USS Kearsarge* offshore, then to Conakry.
May 31	Ghana and Guinea airlift troops to support Nigerian contingents in Freetown. Three hundred foreign nationals located in Sierra Leone are evacuated to a French naval vessel.
June 1	A Nigerian attempt to oust the junta fails after Nigerian troops and 800 foreigners are trapped in the Mammy Yoko Hotel, on fire and under siege by junta forces. An ICRC representative negotiates their safe passage. Nigerians move Sankoh from the Sheraton Hotel in Abuja to a local security installation.
June 1	Major Koroma invites the RUF to join the junta. The RUF enters Freetown as the merged "People's Army." Koroma forms AFRC ruling council with RUF leader Sankoh as vice chairman.
June 2	U.S. Marines evacuate an additional 1,200 foreigners, including those from the Mammy Yoko Hotel, to Conakry. The OAU Summit in Harare condemns the coup, and calls for Kabbah's immediate restoration.
June 3	AFRC/RUF forces are in control of Freetown. Nigeria airlifts hundreds of troops from Monrovia to Lungi.
June 27	Economic Community of West African States (ECOWAS) foreign ministers meeting in Conakry adopt a three-point plan to persuade the AFRC/RUF junta to step down: dialogue, an embargo, and if necessary the use of force. A Committee of Four (C-4) is appointed.
June 30	Two thousand RUF fighters arrive in Freetown to support the AFRC.
July 18–19	ECOWAS Committee of Four (composed of the foreign ministers of Nigeria, Côte d'Ivoire, Guinea, and Ghana) meets in Abidjan with AFRC/RUF rep-

resentatives to try to negotiate a return to constitutional rule.

July 19   Koroma announces on Sierra Leone Broadcasting Corporation Radio that he intends to remain in office until 2001. Negotiations collapse. ECOWAS imposes an embargo on military supplies to the junta. The Nigerians mount a naval blockade of Freetown.

August 29   The ECOWAS Heads of State Summit in Abuja adopts sanctions on petroleum products, arms imports, and international travel of AFRC/RUF leaders. The C-4 is expanded to include Liberia, making it C-5. ECOMOG's official mandate is extended to include Sierra Leone.

September 25   The UN accredits President Kabbah as leader of the Sierra Leone delegation to the UN General Assembly.

October 8   UN Security Council Resolution 1132 is adopted, establishing an embargo on weapons and other military equipment, petroleum, and petroleum products on Sierra Leone. ECOWAS is empowered to enforce the embargo under Chapters VII and VIII of the UN Charter.

October 23   In negotiations in Conakry between the junta and ECOWAS C-5, the AFRC/RUF agree to restore Kabbah to office within six months, that is, by April 22, 1998.

November 12   Nigerian foreign minister Ikimi, on behalf of ECOWAS, requests the Security Council to provide military and technical assistance for ECOMOG.

November 25   Special representative of the UN Secretary-General Francis Okelo, ECOWAS executive secretary Lansana Kouyate, and ECOMOG force commander Victor Malu visit Freetown. Staged demonstrations and demands for Sankoh's release imperil the Conakry Accord.

December   Tim Spicer of Sandline International and Kabbah meet. Spicer proposes a military plan to help restore civilian rule. A Thai businessman resident in Canada, Rakesh Saxena, offers to finance the plan. He pays Sandline $1.5 million for the first installment but is subsequently arrested by the

Canadian government for passport fraud. The scheme collapses for lack of funds, although some arms intended for the Nigerians and Kamajohs do reach Freetown.

December 9   ECOMOG, AFRC, RUF, and civil defense groups agree on a fourteen-point disarmament plan.

1998 January 18   Kamajoh militiamen capture the diamond-mining town of Tongo, depriving the AFRC of a large source of income. The Kamajoh offensive in the southeast is backed by the Nigerians, with Sandline reportedly providing intelligence and logistical support. President Taylor accuses Nigerian troops of transiting South African mercenaries across his territory. At the C-5 briefing of the UN Security Council, Foreign Minister Ikimi disclaims knowledge of an ECOMOG offensive. ECOMOG at the same time launches an assault on Freetown.

January 18–25 Fierce fighting erupts in Freetown.

February 15   The AFRC/RUF junta flees and Nigerian troops take control of the city. The UK, Sweden, and other Security Council members express disappointment that ECOWAS did not attempt to inform the Security Council in advance.

February 16   ECOMOG announces it has taken control of the Freetown peninsula.

February 20   ECOMOG arrests former president Joseph Momoh in Freetown.

March 2   At the Commonwealth Ministerial Action Group meeting in London, British minister of state for Africa Tony Lloyd insists that Nigerian action in Freetown is illegal, but Ghanaian foreign minister Victor Gbeho says it is fully backed by ECOWAS and urges Commonwealth support.

March 6   The British Foreign Office is implicated for alleged involvement in Sandline's plan to ship weapons to Sierra Leone in violation of UN Security Council Resolution 1132 prohibiting all arms imports. This is followed within days by an official investigation.

March 10   Accompanied by General Abacha of Nigeria, President Conteh of Guinea, and other high-ranking officials, Kabbah returns to Freetown and is reinstated as president. British Customs and Excise launch an investigation into Sandline's role

	in Sierra Leone, focusing on illegal arms shipments.
March 16	The UN Security Council adopts Resolution 1156, terminating the embargo of petroleum and petroleum products on Sierra Leone. Kabbah declares a national state of emergency.
March 20	President Kabbah announces formation of his third cabinet.
March 26	Sierra Leone's parliament convenes for the first time since the coup and ratifies the state of emergency.
March 30	ECOMOG forces move into Kono District, the last AFRC/RUF stronghold.
April 16	President Kabbah places ECOMOG task force commander Maxwell Khobe, promoted to brigadier general and Sierra Leone chief of Defense Staff, in charge of Sierra Leone's internal security.
April 17	The UN Security Council approves Resolution 1162, authorizing deployment of ten military liaison and security advisory personnel to Sierra Leone to report on the military situation and develop a plan for further UN deployment if necessary.
April 24	Sandline's solicitors write a letter to Foreign Secretary Robin Cook arguing that, from the beginning, both Whitehall and High Commissioner Penfold in Freetown were aware of Sandline's actions.
April 28	President Kabbah announces that the Civil Defense Force (CDF), made up of traditional militias, have been placed under the control of ECOMOG.
May 6	Trials against alleged junta plotters are instituted. The World Bank announces $100 million in emergency aid for Sierra Leone.
May 18	Foreign Secretary Robin Cook discloses that Britain financed Radio Democracy, FM 98.1, which the exiled government of President Kabbah used to mobilize support in Sierra Leone.
May 20	ECOMOG announces that all provincial capitals in Sierra Leone are under its "effective control."
May 22–30	ECOMOG force commander Major-General Timothy Shelpidi offers amnesty to all AFRC/RUF members who come forward and surrender. The government follows suit.

June 5	The UN Security Council approves Resolution 1171. The resolution lifts the arms embargo for the Sierra Leone government and ECOMOG but retains the embargo against "nongovernmental forces." It also places a travel sanction on the former junta and the RUF.
June 8	Abacha dies suddenly in Abuja under mysterious circumstances.
June 17	ECOMOG completes the screening of 5,000 volunteers for the new Sierra Leone Army. Fifteen hundred of the volunteers are reported to be soldiers who surrendered to ECOMOG during the period of amnesty.
July 2	In Abuja, Kabbah and Taylor (Liberia) sign an agreement on reciprocal confidence-building measures in the presence of UN Secretary-General Annan and ECOWAS chairman Abubakr.
July 9	Vice President Demby announces amnesty for all child soldiers.
July 11	ECOMOG captures Kailahun, the location of the RUF headquarters, but RUF forces evade capture and move north and west.
July 13	UN Security Council Resolution 1181 is adopted, establishing the UN Observer Mission in Sierra Leone (UNOMSIL) with seventy military observers for an initial period of six months.
July 14	ECOMOG decides to transfer most of the forces remaining in Monrovia to Freetown.
July 20	President Kabbah visits Monrovia at the request of President Taylor to attend the Liberian National Reconciliation Conference.
July 25	Sankoh is returned to Sierra Leone from Nigeria.
July 30	Secretary-General Annan convenes a special conference in New York on Sierra Leone to raise funds for ECOMOG operations; disarmament, demobilization, and reintegration (DDR); emergency relief; and reconstruction.
August 17	The RUF announces the commencement of a terror campaign directed against civilians should Sankoh remain in government custody.
September	ECOMOG forces and Kamajoh militia capture four eastern towns (Joru, Mande-Kalema, Tokunbu, and Nyama) in a joint surprise attack.

	September 2	Kabbah outlines plans for a new army composed of 5,000 troops under civilian control.
	Late September	ECOMOG fighter-bombers destroy six RUF bases in Kailahun District.
	October 1	The CDF, with ECOMOG support, launches offensives against rebel strongholds in Kailahun.
	October 19	Twenty-four military officers are executed for their role in the AFRC/RUF junta. Ten others have their sentences commuted to life imprisonment.
	October 23	Sankoh is sentenced to death after a jury finds him guilty on seven counts of treason. The jury rejects Sankoh's argument that he was granted amnesty under the 1996 Abidjan Peace Agreement.
	October 31	ECOWAS heads of state meeting in Abuja agree to strengthen the ECOMOG force in Sierra Leone. Benin, Côte d'Ivoire, Mali, and Niger offer to contribute troops or medical supplies depending on availability of international logistics.
	October 31	Chief of Defense Maxwell Khobe accuses Liberia's National Patriotic Front of continuing to provide support to AFRC/RUF elements.
	December	Foreign personnel are evacuated from Freetown as the security situation deteriorates.
1999	January 6	The AFRC/RUF reenters Freetown by force in a major setback for ECOMOG. Massive destruction, loss of life, and amputations take place in the eastern sector.
	February 27	In Nigeria, General Olusegun Obasanjo is elected as the first civilian president since 1983. Internal pressures quickly develop for the reduction and ultimate withdrawal of Nigerian forces from Sierra Leone.
	April	Sankoh is allowed to go to Lomé, Togo, for consultations with his commanders and associates on renewed negotiations.
	May 18	In the presence of U.S. special envoy Jesse Jackson and Togolese president Eyadema, Kabbah and Sankoh sign a cease-fire agreement in Lomé.
	May 25	Negotiations open on new peace agreement. The RUF demands a blanket amnesty and eight cabinet positions. The two sides agree to renew most of the provisions of the Abidjan Agreement including

demobilization and disarmament, and the RUF's transformation into a political party.

May 26   After delays, direct talks between the Sierra Leone government and the RUF finally get under way in Lomé, Togo.

May 29   Obasanjo is inaugurated as civilian president of Nigeria.

June 5   The Guinean army sends a "punitive expedition" into Sierra Leone, killing about 100 rebels of the Sierra Leonean People's Army (SPA), a breakaway faction of the RUF, in response to a recent raid on the Guinean town of Tassin where there were indications of further plans to attack Guinean towns.

June 10   Several ministers threaten a cabinet revolt if President Kabbah accedes to RUF demands for power sharing in a transitional government.

June 24   United Nations High Commissioner for Human Rights Mary Robinson signs a nine-point Human Rights Manifesto in Freetown, calling for the establishment of a truth and reconciliation commission to investigate war atrocities.

June 26   A three-member RUF delegation headed by People's War Council chairman Solomon Y. B. Rogers leaves Lomé for Liberia late Saturday aboard a Nigerian plane. The delegation, which was accompanied by mediators from Nigeria, Togo, and Liberia, proceeds to Sierra Leone to submit a draft peace agreement to RUF commanders on the ground.

July 1   Sankoh rejects an initial peace agreement that provided only four ministerial and three deputy-ministerial cabinet posts to the RUF.

July 7   The Lomé Peace Agreement is signed by President Kabbah and Corporal Foday Sankoh. The UN Security Council welcomes the agreement, calling it "a significant achievement for all concerned and a historic turning point for Sierra Leone and its people."

July 10   Thousands of civilians and rebels emerge from the bush in search of food, overwhelming current humanitarian capabilities.

July 11   Foday Sankoh flies to Algeria to attend the OAU Summit.

July 16	The Sierra Leone parliament votes unanimously to ratify the peace accord.
July 23	Ninety-eight people convicted of collaborating with the AFRC junta are pardoned.
July 27	Hundreds of displaced teachers demonstrate in front of the Ministry of Education after it defaulted on payment of salary arrears of up to eleven months.
July 28	At a donor conference for Sierra Leone, the UK pledges $7.1 million for training and equipping a national army.
October 3	Sankoh and Koroma return to Freetown.
October 18	U.S. Secretary of State Albright meets with Kabbah, Sankoh, and Koroma in Freetown.
October 22	UN Security Council Resolution 1270 establishes the UN Mission in Sierra Leone (UNAMSIL), authorizing a peacekeeping force of up to 6,000 troops under Chapter VII "to ensure the security of movement of its personnel and, within its capabilities and areas of deployment, to afford protection to civilians under immediate threat of violence, taking into account the responsibilities of the Sierra Leone government and ECOMOG." Half of the 6,000 troops are expected to be contributed by ECOWAS countries. The balance of troops are expected from Kenya, India, and Zambia.
November 1	UN Special Envoy Francis Okelo notes that the UN was "extremely concerned" with the severity of recent cease-fire violations. These include active combat, movement of troops and weapons, human rights abuses against civilians, systematic assaults of humanitarian personnel, and continued detention of abductees.
November 2	President Kabbah forms his new cabinet, including three ministers and four deputy ministers representing the RUF and AFRC.
November 17	Nigerian diplomat Oluyemi Adeniji is appointed as UN Special Representative to Sierra Leone, to succeed Francis Okelo.
November 20	General Vijay Kumar Jetley of India is selected to lead the United Nations Mission in Sierra Leone.
November 22	The RUF registers with the Interim National Electoral Commission as a political party.

November 30	Sierra Leone and UN officials welcome the first contingent of Kenyan troops serving in UNAMSIL, who will number 820.
December 10	Two Médecins Sans Frontières workers are abducted by RUF commander Sam Bockarie, continuing a trend of kidnappings of humanitarian personnel. In this case, Bockarie reportedly took the two European workers to bring international attention to his fear that Foday Sankoh was planning his assassination.
December 15	National Commission for Disarmament reports that only 23 percent or 10,557 of an estimated 45,000 soldiers were disarmed by the December 15 deadline.
December 16	Sam Bockarie "Maskita," RUF field commander, flees to Liberia, revealing tensions within the RUF. It is rumored that he has been rallying his contingents against the Lomé accords and executed several RUF officers in his flight. Charles Taylor later acknowledges that he has met with Bockarie in Liberia.
December 29	Foday Sankoh presents a paper to President Kabbah and the international community entitled "Violations of the Lomé Peace Accord," warning of an immediate crisis in the implementation of the agreement if urgent action is not taken to make progress on key provisions.
2000 January 12	Secretary-General Annan calls for the expansion of UNAMSIL from 6,000 to 11,100 troops.
January 19	The Sierra Leone Parliament approves legislation for an Anti-Corruption Bureau with wide powers to investigate alleged or suspected corruption in all public departments.
January 23	Sankoh, as chairman of the Commission for the Management of Stategic Resources, National Reconstruction and Development, announces a moratorium on all diamond mining in Sierra Leone. He warns that anyone caught mining illicitly will be arrested and prosecuted and anyone formerly carrying licenses must reapply with the CMRRD. Photos a month later show that diamond-mining activity in rebel-held areas has not ceased.

February 2	United Nations Human Rights Monitoring Mission reports that former rebel fighters are continuing to loot, rape, and mutilate civilians.
February 7	The UN Security Council adopts Resolution 1289 increasing the authorized strength of UNAMSIL to 11,100 troops.
February 21	Sankoh is expelled from South Africa after the UN Security Council Sanctions Committee on Sierra Leone informs the governments of South Africa and Côte d'Ivoire that Sankoh's visit is in violation of an international travel ban imposed in 1997.
February 23	The parliament approves draft legislation for the establishment of a Truth and Reconciliation Commission.
February 24	UN peacekeepers stand off after one of many confrontations with the RUF, which continues to prevent the UN mission from taking up positions in eastern Sierra Leone.
February 29	De Beers, controlling the sales of 70–80 percent of the world's diamonds, announces that it will guarantee that any uncut gems it sells through the Central Selling Organization will not originate in rebel-held territories.
March 3	The presidents of Liberia, Guinea, and Sierra Leone leave a mini-summit in Bamako, Mali, pledging that "no country will be used as a base to destabilize another country."
March 21	President Kabbah swears in members of the new Electoral Commission to organize the presidential and parliamentary elections to be held in 2001.
March 27	Thousands march through Freetown protesting the slow pace of the disarmament process.
March 30	Human Rights Watch calls on Burkina Faso's President Blaise Compaore to order an independent investigation into charges that his country facilitated illegal arms transfers to the rebel forces.
April 4	ECOMOG resumes its troop reduction plan. Remaining ECOMOG troops are expected to be subsumed under UN command. Twenty thousand teachers return to work after a week-long strike over unpaid salaries. Problems continue in staffing and payment in several sectors of the civil service.

April 18   Sierra Leone Chief of Defense Staff/Brigadier-General Maxwell Khobe dies in Nigeria due to a series of complications from an earlier shrapnel wound.

April 25   RUF fighters surround a disarmament reception center in Magburaka, forcing UN peacekeepers to dismantle the camp in a continuing trend of non-cooperation with the disarmament process.

April 26   UNAMSIL gains a presence in nine of Sierra Leone's twelve districts but has not yet managed to deploy in eastern Kono District where the RUF is strongest. Nigerian troops continue to head for home.

May 2   The ECOMOG force completes its withdrawal from Sierra Leone.

May 4   The bodies of four Kenyan peacekeepers are recovered and sent home for burial.

May 6   UNAMSIL loses contact with another 200 peacekeepers, bringing the number held by the RUF to around 500.

May 7   RUF rebels shoot down a UN helicopter. Two helicopters were shot at, both carrying food and supplies for UN peacekeepers surrounded by rebels in Makeni and Magburaka. One was able to pick up three wounded Kenyan peacekeepers. Evacuation of foreigners begins.

May 8   An estimated 30,000 demonstrators, organized by civil society groups to condemn the RUF detention of UN peacekeepers, march toward Sankoh's residence. Nigerian UNAMSIL troops fire into the air to disperse the crowd. The RUF opens fire, killing seventeen and injuring many others. During the fighting, Sankoh escapes out the back of his house and goes into hiding.

May 13   Six British warships take up position in Sierra Leonean waters.

May 15   The Executive Secretary of the National Commission for Disarmament, Demobilization, and Reintegration reveals that the NCDDR program has come to a "temporary halt" due to RUF attacks against the UN peacekeeping forces and the group's unwillingness to disarm according to a shared timetable. British forces secure Lungi Airport.

May 17	Foday Sankoh is captured near his residence in the early hours of the morning. He is arrested and then stripped and paraded through the streets by the crowd before ending up in government custody.
May 22	The bodies of what are suspected to be UN peace-keepers, including four Zambians and one Nigerian, are found at Rogberi Junction, raising concerns over the continued holding of UN hostages. Secretary-General Annan recommends the increase of the peacekeeping force from 13,000 to 16,500 troops.
May 24	Two journalists—Kurt Schork of Reuters and Gil Moreno of the Associated Press—are killed in an ambush by the RUF near Rogberi Junction. Four Sierra Leone army soldiers are also killed in the attack.
May 25	UNAMSIL spokesperson David Wimhurst states that Foday Sankoh is no longer a "credible" negotiating partner for continued dialogue involved in the peace process.
May 26	President Kabbah announces that Foday Sankoh will be tried for crimes committed since the July 7 Lomé Agreement.
May 29	The ECOWAS Summit in Abuja approves a proposal to send an additional 3,000 troops to Sierra Leone. The regional leaders also call for UNAMSIL's mandate to be changed from peace-keeping to peace enforcement and for the force to be headed by a West African.
May 30	Of the UN peacekeepers abducted by the RUF, 467 are released; 258 UN personnel remain surrounded by RUF troops.
June 3	Liberia offers to contribute troops to the proposed 3,000-man ECOWAS peacekeeping contingent to Sierra Leone.
June 7	RUF Field Commander General Issa Sesay meets with UNAMSIL Field Commander Major Punia, indicating that his troops want to return to the peace process.
June 10	A British training team of military trainers and soldiers to provide security starts arriving in Freetown. The team begins training 1,000 soldiers of the new Sierra Leone Army.

June 12	The Israel Diamond Exchange states that it will revoke membership of any diamond dealer who knowingly sells "conflict diamonds" that have originated from rebels in Sierra Leone, Angola, or the Democratic Republic of Congo.
June 13	The European Union decides to suspend EU 50 million ($48 million) in development aid to Liberia until its support for the RUF ceases.
June 15	The British operation, code named "Operation Palliser," formally ends at midnight as the British soldiers are sent home. Military advisers remain to work with UNAMSIL and the Sierra Leone Army.
June 18	*The Washington Post* reports that the Liberian government has resupplied and reinforced RUF rebels in eastern Sierra Leone, preparing them to fight rather than allow the UN to take over diamond-mining areas under their control.
June 20	U.S. Ambassador to the UN Richard Holbrooke calls for an international tribunal to try rebel leaders accused of war crimes in Sierra Leone. Great Britain proposes an embargo on diamonds from Sierra Leone, most of which are smuggled through Liberia.
June 21	ECOWAS leaders meet at the UN to discuss the current proposals on Sierra Leone. There are estimates of 500,000 Sierra Leonean and Liberian refugees now in Guinea.
July 5	The United Nations Security Council adopts Resolution 1306 to impose an embargo on the sale of rough Sierra Leonean diamonds. The British-sponsored resolution makes it illegal to buy Sierra Leonean diamonds unless they are accompanied by a certificate of origin from the government. Until such a certification system is in place, the resolution will ban all diamonds originating in Sierra Leone, except those passing through official government channels.
July 10	The Sierra Leone government orders the "West Side Boys"—ex-SLA soldiers loyal to AFRC leader Johnny Paul Koroma—to report to Masiaka on Monday and Tuesday to be disarmed by UNAMSIL.
July 19	Diamond industry leaders meet at the World

	Diamond Congress in Antwerp, Belgium, and adopt measures to clamp down on the illegal trade in "conflict diamonds." The industry will adopt a certification system to track diamonds from where they are mined to the international diamond trading centers. The measure also provides tough penalties against dealers who break UN embargoes on diamond dealing with rebels in Sierra Leone.
August 8	Johnny Paul Koroma formally disassociates himself from renegade soldiers of the AFRC, including the West Side Boys militia.
August 14	The United Nations Security Council adopts Resolution 1315 supporting the creation of a special tribunal to try "persons who bear the greatest responsibility" for serious crimes under Sierra Leonean and international law. The resolution authorizes Secretary-General Annan to negotiate an agreement with the Sierra Leone government to create an independent special court to try crimes against humanity, war crimes, and other serious violations of both international humanitarian and Sierra Leonean law.
August 15	Justice Minister and Attorney-General Solomon Berewa announces that RUF leader Foday Sankoh will be tried before the tribunal.
August 21	The RUF names General Issa Sesay to replace Foday Sankoh as leader of the movement.
August 26	Eleven soldiers from Britain's Royal Irish Regiment and one Sierra Leone Army soldier are missing, amid reports they were abducted by former West Side Boys.
August 28	Secretary-General Annan recommends that UNAMSIL's strength be increased to 20,500 to enhance the force's operational structure and overall effectiveness, and to allow deployment in key areas.
August 30	Five of the British soldiers are released. The West Side Boys issue a statement saying they distrust the government, and will not disarm until their demands are met.
September 10	British forces, in a surprise attack, free remaining British and Sierra Leonean hostages, inflicting serious casualties among the captors.

NOTE

This chronology is taken from several sources including *Africa Confidential,* Sierra Leone News, and wire service reports.

Appendix 2

The Lomé Peace Agreement

**The Government of the Republic of Sierra Leone
and the Revolutionary United Front of Sierra Leone (RUF/SL)**

Having met in Lomé, Togo, from May 25, 1999, to July 7, 1999, under the auspices of the current chairman of ECOWAS, President Gnassingbe Eyadema;

Recalling earlier initiatives undertaken by the countries of the subregion and the international community, aimed at bringing about a negotiated settlement of the conflict in Sierra Leone, and culminating in the Abidjan Peace Agreement of November 30, 1996, and the ECOWAS Peace Plan of October 23, 1997;

Moved by the imperative need to meet the desire of the people of Sierra Leone for a definitive settlement of the fratricidal war in their country and for genuine national unity and reconciliation;

Committed to promoting full respect for human rights and humanitarian law;

Committed to promoting popular participation in the governance of the country and the advancement of democracy in a sociopolitical framework free of inequality, nepotism, and corruption;

Concerned with the socioeconomic well-being of all the people of Sierra Leone;

Determined to foster mutual trust and confidence between themselves;

Determined to establish sustainable peace and security; to pledge forthwith, to settle all past, present, and future differences and grievances by peaceful means; and to refrain from the threat and use of armed force to bring about any change in Sierra Leone;

Reaffirming the conviction that sovereignty belongs to the people, and that government derives all its powers, authority, and legitimacy from the people;

Recognizing the imperative that the children of Sierra Leone, especially those affected by armed conflict, in view of their vulnerability, are entitled to special care and the protection of their inherent right to life, survival, and development, in accordance with the provisions of the International Convention on the Rights of the Child;

Guided by the Declaration in the Final Communiqué of the Meeting in Lomæ of the ministers of foreign affairs of ECOWAS of May 25, 1999, in which they stressed the importance of democracy as a factor of regional peace and security, and as essential to the socioeconomic development of ECOWAS member states; and in which they pledged their commitment to the consolidation of democracy and respect of human rights while reaffirming the need for all member states to consolidate their democratic base, observe the principles of good governance and good economic management in order to ensure the emergence and development of a democratic culture that takes into account the interests of the peoples of West Africa;

Recommitting themselves to the total observance and compliance with the Cease-Fire Agreement signed in Lomæ on May 18, 1999, and appended as Annex 1 until the signing of the present Peace Agreement.

Hereby agree as follows:

PART ONE: CESSATION OF HOSTILITIES

Article I: Cease-Fire

The armed conflict between the government of Sierra Leone and the RUF/SL is hereby ended with immediate effect. Accordingly, the two sides shall ensure that a total and permanent cessation of hostilities is observed forthwith.

Article II: Cease-Fire Monitoring

1. A Cease-Fire Monitoring Committee (hereinafter termed the CMC) to be chaired by the United Nations Observer Mission in Sierra Leone (hereinafter termed UNOMSIL) with representatives of the government of Sierra Leone, RUF/SL, the Civil Defence Forces (hereinafter termed the CDF) and ECOMOG shall be established at provincial and district levels with immediate effect to monitor, verify, and report all violations of the cease-fire.

2. A Joint Monitoring Commission (hereinafter termed the JMC) shall

be established at the national level to be chaired by UNOMSIL with representatives of the government of Sierra Leone, RUF/SL, CDF, and ECOMOG. The JMC shall receive, investigate, and take appropriate action on reports of violations of the cease-fire from the CMC. The parties agree to the definition of cease-fire violations as contained in Annex 2, which constitutes an integral part of the present agreement.

3. The parties shall seek the assistance of the international community in providing funds and other logistics to enable the JMC to carry out its mandate.

PART TWO: GOVERNANCE

The government of Sierra Leone and the RUF/SL, recognizing the right of the people of Sierra Leone to live in peace, and desirous of finding a transitional mechanism to incorporate the RUF/SL into governance within the spirit and letter of the constitution, agree to the following formulas for structuring the government for the duration of the period before the next elections, as prescribed by the constitution, managing scarce public resources for the benefit of the development of the people of Sierra Leone and sharing the responsibility of implementing the peace. Each of these formulas (not in priority order) is contained in a separate article of this part of the present agreement; and may be further detailed in protocols annexed to it.

Article III—Transformation of the RUF/SL into a Political Party

Article IV—Enabling Members of the RUF/SL to Hold Public Office

Article V—Enabling the RUF/SL to Join a Broad-Based Government of National Unity Through Cabinet Appointments

Article VI—Commission for the Consolidation of Peace

Article VII—Commission for the Management of Strategic Resources, National Reconstruction and Development

Article VIII—Council of Elders and Religious Leaders.

Article III: Transformation of the RUF/SL into a Political Party

1. The government of Sierra Leone shall accord every facility to the RUF/SL to transform itself into a political party and enter the mainstream of the democratic process. To that end:

2. Immediately upon the signing of the present agreement, the RUF/SL shall commence to organize itself to function as a political movement, with the rights, privileges, and duties accorded to all political parties

in Sierra Leone. These include the freedom to publish, unhindered access to the media, freedom of association, freedom of expression, freedom of assembly, and the right to mobilize and associate freely.

3. Within a period of thirty days, following the signing of the present agreement, the necessary legal steps shall be taken by the government of Sierra Leone to enable the RUF/SL to register as a political party.

4. The parties shall approach the international community with a view to mobilizing resources for the purposes of enabling the RUF/SL to function as a political party. These resources may include but shall not be limited to:

(i) Setting up a trust fund;

(ii) Training for RUF/SL membership in party organization and functions; and

(iii) Providing any other assistance necessary for achieving the goals of this section.

Article IV: Enabling Members of the RUF/SL to Hold Public Office

1. The government of Sierra Leone shall take the necessary steps to enable those RUF/SL members nominated by the RUF/SL to hold public office, within the time-frames agreed and contained in the present agreement for the integration of the various bodies named herein.

2. Accordingly, necessary legal steps shall be taken by the government of Sierra Leone, within a period of fourteen days following the signing of the present agreement, to amend relevant laws and regulations that may constitute an impediment or bar to RUF/SL and AFRC personnel holding public office.

3. Within seven days of the removal of any such legal impediments, both parties shall meet to discuss and agree on the appointment of RUF/SL members to positions in parastatals, diplomacy, and any other public sector.

Article V: Enabling the RUF/SL to Join a Broad-Based Government of National Unity Through Cabinet Appointments

1. The government of Sierra Leone shall accord every opportunity to the RUF/SL to join a broad-based government of national unity through cabinet appointments. To that end:

2. The chairmanship of the board of the Commission for the Management of Strategic Resources, National Reconstruction, and Development (CMRRD) as provided for in Article VII of the present agreement shall be offered to the leader of the RUF/SL, Corporal Foday Sankoh. For this pur-

pose he shall enjoy the status of vice president and shall therefore be answerable only to the president of Sierra Leone.

3. The government of Sierra Leone shall give ministerial positions to the RUF/SL in a moderately expanded cabinet of eighteen, bearing in mind that the interests of other political parties and civil society organizations should also be taken into account, as follows:

(i) One of the senior cabinet appointments such as finance, foreign affairs, and justice;

(ii) Three other cabinet positions.

4. In addition, the Government of Sierra Leone shall, in the same spirit, make available to the RUF/SL the following senior government positions: Four posts of Deputy Minister.

5. Within a period of fourteen days following the signing of the present Agreement, the necessary steps shall be taken by the Government of Sierra Leone to remove any legal impediments that may prevent RUF/SL members from holding cabinet and other positions.

Article VI: Commission for the Consolidation of Peace

1. A Commission for the Consolidation of Peace (hereinafter termed the CCP), shall be established within two weeks of the signing of the present agreement to implement a postconflict program that ensures reconciliation and the welfare of all parties to the conflict, especially the victims of war. The CCP shall have the overall goal and responsibility for supervising and monitoring the implementation of and compliance with the provisions of the present agreement relative to the promotion of national reconciliation and the consolidation of peace.

2. The CCP shall ensure that all structures for national reconciliation and the consolidation of peace already in existence and those provided for in the present Agreement are operational and given the necessary resources for realizing their respective mandates. These structures shall comprise:

(i) the Commission for the Management of Strategic Resources, National Reconstruction, and Development;

(ii) the Joint Monitoring Commission;

(iii) the Provincial and District Cease-Fire Monitoring Committees;

(iv) the Committee for the Release of Prisoners of War and Non-Combatants;

(v) the Committee for Humanitarian Assistance;

(vi) the National Commission on Disarmament, Demobilization, and Reintegration;

(vii) the National Commission for Resettlement, Rehabilitation, and Reconstruction;

(viii) the Human Rights Commission; and

(ix) the Truth and Reconciliation Commission.

3. The CCP shall have the right to inspect any activity or site connected with the implementation of the present agreement.

4. The CCP shall have full powers to organize its work in any manner it deems appropriate and to appoint any group or subcommittee that it deems necessary in the discharge of its functions.

5. The commission shall be composed of the following members:

(i) Two representatives of the civil society;

(ii) One representative each named by the government, the RUF/SL, and the parliament.

6. The CCP shall have its own offices, adequate communication facilities, and secretarial support staff.

7. Recommendations for improvements or modifications shall be made to the president of Sierra Leone for appropriate action. Likewise, failures of the structures to perform their assigned duties shall also be brought to the attention of the president.

8. Disputes arising out of the preceding paragraph shall be brought to the Council of Elders and Religious Leaders for resolution, as specified in Article VIII of the present agreement.

9. Should protocols be needed in furtherance of any provision in the present agreement, the CCP shall have the responsibility for their preparation.

10. The mandate of the CCP shall terminate at the end of the next general elections.

Article VII: Commission for the Management of Strategic Resources, National Reconstruction and Development

1. Given the emergency situation facing the country, the parties agree that the government shall exercise full control over the exploitation of gold, diamonds, and other resources, for the benefit of the people of Sierra Leone. Accordingly, a Commission for the Management of Strategic Resources, National Reconstruction, and Development (hereinafter termed the CMRRD) shall be established and charged with the responsibility of securing and monitoring the legitimate exploitation of Sierra Leone's gold and diamonds, and other resources that are determined to be of strategic importance for national security and welfare as well as cater for postwar rehabilitation and reconstruction, as provided for under Article XXVIII of the present agreement.

2. The government shall take the necessary legal action within a period not exceeding two weeks from the signing of the present agreement to the effect that all exploitation, sale, export, or any other transaction of gold

and diamonds shall be forbidden except those sanctioned by the CMRRD. All previous concessions shall be null and void.

3. The CMRRD shall authorize licensing of artisanal production of diamonds and gold, in accordance with prevailing laws and regulations. All gold and diamonds extracted or otherwise sourced from any Sierra Leonean territory shall be sold to the government.

4. The CMRRD shall ensure, through the appropriate authorities, the security of the areas covered under this article, and shall take all necessary measures against unauthorized exploitation.

5. For the export or local resale of gold and diamonds by the government, the CMRRD shall authorize a buying and selling agreement with one or more reputable international and specialized mineral companies. All exports of Sierra Leonean gold and diamonds shall be transacted by the government, under these agreements.

6. The proceeds from the transactions of gold and diamonds shall be public monies that shall enter a special treasury account to be spent exclusively on the development of the people of Sierra Leone, with appropriations for public education, public health, infrastructural development, and compensation for incapacitated war victims as well as postwar rehabilitation and reconstruction. Priority spending shall go to rural areas.

7. The government shall, if necessary, seek the assistance and cooperation of other governments and their instruments of law enforcement to detect and facilitate the prosecution of violations of this article.

8. The management of other natural resources shall be reviewed by the CMRRD to determine if their regulation is a matter of national security and welfare, and recommend appropriate policy to the government.

9. The functions of the Ministry of Mines shall continue to be carried out by the current authorized ministry. However, in respect of strategic mineral resources, the CMRRD shall be an autonomous body in carrying out its duties concerning the regulation of Sierra Leone's strategic natural resources.

10. All agreements and transactions referred to in this article shall be subject to full public disclosure and records of all correspondence, negotiations, business transactions, and any other matters related to exploitation, management, local or international marketing, and any other matter shall be public documents.

11. The commission shall issue monthly reports, including the details of all the transactions related to gold and diamonds, and other licenses or concessions of natural resources, and its own administrative costs.

12. The commission shall be governed by a board whose chairmanship shall be offered to the leader of the RUF/SL, Corporal Foday Sankoh. The board shall also comprise:

(i) Two representatives of the government appointed by the president;

(ii) Two representatives of the political party to be formed by the RUF/SL;

(iii) Three representatives of the civil society; and

(iv) Two representatives of other political parties appointed by parliament.

13. The government shall take the required administrative actions to implement the commitments made in the present agreement; and in the case of enabling legislation, it shall draft and submit to parliament within thirty days of the signature of the present agreement, the relevant bills for their enactment into law.

14. The government commits itself to propose and support an amendment to the constitution to make the exploitation of gold and diamonds the legitimate domain of the people of Sierra Leone, and to determine that the proceeds be used for the development of Sierra Leone, particularly public education, public health, infrastructure development, and compensation of incapacitated war victims as well as postwar reconstruction and development.

Article VIII: Council of Elders and Religious Leaders

1. The signatories agree to refer any conflicting differences of interpretation of this article or any other article of the present agreement or its protocols, to a Council of Elders and Religious Leaders comprised as follows:

(i) Two members appointed by the Inter-Religious Council;

(ii) One member each appointed by the government and the RUF/SL; and

(iii) One member appointed by ECOWAS.

2. The council shall designate its own chairperson from among its members. All of its decisions shall be taken by the concurrence of at least four members, and shall be binding and public, provided that an aggrieved party may appeal to the supreme court.

PART THREE: OTHER POLITICAL ISSUES

The third part of the present agreement consists of the following articles:

Article IX—Pardon and Amnesty
Article X—Review of the Present Constitution
Article XI—Date of Next Elections
Article XII—National Electoral Commission

Article IX: Pardon and Amnesty

1. In order to bring lasting peace to Sierra Leone, the government of Sierra Leone shall take appropriate legal steps to grant Corporal Foday Sankoh absolute and free pardon.

2. After the signing of the present agreement, the government of Sierra Leone shall also grant absolute and free pardon and reprieve to all combatants and collaborators in respect of anything done by them in pursuit of their objectives, up to the time of the signing of the present agreement.

3. To consolidate the peace and promote the cause of national reconciliation, the government of Sierra Leone shall ensure that no official or judicial action is taken against any member of the RUF/SL, ex-AFRC, ex-SLA, or CDF in respect of anything done by them in pursuit of their objectives as members of those organizations, since March 1991, up to the time of the signing of the present agreement. In addition, legislative and other measures necessary to guarantee immunity to former combatants, exiles, and other persons currently outside the country for reasons related to the armed conflict shall be adopted ensuring the full exercise of their civil and political rights, with a view to their reintegration within a framework of full legality.

Article X: Review of the Present Constitution

In order to ensure that the 1991 Constitution of Sierra Leone represents the needs and aspirations of the people of Sierra Leone and that no constitutional or any other legal provision prevents the implementation of the present agreement, the government of Sierra Leone shall take the necessary steps to establish a Constitutional Review Committee to review the provisions of the present constitution, and where deemed appropriate, recommend revisions and amendments, in accordance with Part V, Section 108 of the Constitution of 1991.

Article XI: Date of Next Elections

The next national elections in Sierra Leone shall be held in accordance with the present constitution of Sierra Leone.

Article XII: National Electoral Commission

1. A new independent National Electoral Commission (hereinafter termed the NEC) shall be set up by the government, not later than three months after the signing of the present agreement.

2. In setting up the new NEC the president shall consult all political

parties, including the RUF/SL, to determine the membership and terms of reference of the commission, paying particular attention to the need for a level playing field in the nation's elections.

3. No member of the NEC shall be eligible for appointment to political office by any government formed as a result of an election he or she was mandated to conduct.

4. The NEC shall request the assistance of the international community, including the UN, the OAU, ECOWAS, and the Commonwealth of Nations, in monitoring the next presidential and parliamentary elections in Sierra Leone.

PART FOUR: POSTCONFLICT MILITARY AND SECURITY ISSUES

1. The government of Sierra Leone and the RUF/SL, recognizing that the maintenance of peace and security is of paramount importance for the achievement of lasting peace in Sierra Leone and for the welfare of its people, have agreed to the following formulas for dealing with postconflict military and security matters. Each of these formulas (not in priority order) is contained in separate articles of this part of the present agreement and may be further detailed in protocols annexed to the agreement.

Article XIII—Transformation and New Mandate of ECOMOG

Article XIV—New Mandate of UNOMSIL

Article XV—Security Guarantees for Peace Monitors

Article XVI—Encampment, Disarmament, Demobilization and Reintegration

Article XVII—Restructuring and Training of the Sierra Leone Armed Forces

Article XVIII—Withdrawal of Mercenaries

Article XIX—Notification to Joint Monitoring Commission

Article XX—Notification to Military Commands

Article XIII: Transformation and New Mandate of ECOMOG

1. Immediately upon the signing of the present agreement, the parties shall request ECOWAS to revise the mandate of ECOMOG in Sierra Leone as follows:

(i) Peacekeeping;

(ii) Security of the State of Sierra Leone;

    i. Protection of UNOMSIL.

    ii. Protection of Disarmament, Demobilization and Reintegration personnel.

2. The government shall, immediately upon the signing of the present agreement, request ECOWAS for troop contributions from at least two additional countries. The additional contingents shall be deployed not later than thirty days from the date of signature of the present agreement. The Security Council shall be requested to provide assistance in support of ECOMOG.

3. The parties agree to develop a timetable for the phased withdrawal of ECOMOG, including measures for securing all of the territory of Sierra Leone by the restructured armed forces. The phased withdrawal of ECOMOG will be linked to the phased creation and deployment of the restructured armed forces.

Article XIV: New Mandate of UNOMSIL

1. The UN Security Council is requested to amend the mandate of UNOMSIL to enable it to undertake the various provisions outlined in the present agreement.

Article XV: Security Guarantees for Peace Monitors

1. The government of Sierra Leone and the RUF/SL agree to guarantee the safety, security, and freedom of movement of UNOMSIL military observers throughout Sierra Leone. This guarantee shall be monitored by the Joint Monitoring Commission.

2. The freedom of movement includes complete and unhindered access for UNOMSIL military observers in the conduct of their duties throughout Sierra Leone. Before and during the process of disarmament, demobilization, and reintegration, officers and escorts to be provided by both parties shall be required to facilitate this access.

3. Such freedom of movement and security shall also be accorded to nonmilitary UNOMSIL personnel such as human rights officers in the conduct of their duties. These personnel shall, in most cases, be accompanied by UNOMSIL military observers.

4. The provision of security to be extended shall include United Nations aircraft, vehicles, and other property.

Article XVI: Encampment, Disarmament, Demobilization, and Reintegration

1. A neutral peacekeeping force comprised of UNOMSIL and ECOMOG shall disarm all combatants of the RUF/SL, CDF, SLA, and paramilitary groups. The encampment, disarmament, and demobilization process shall commence within six weeks of the signing of the present agreement in line with the deployment of the neutral peacekeeping force.

2. The present SLA shall be restricted to the barracks and their arms in the armory and their ammunitions in the magazines and placed under constant surveillance by the neutral peacekeeping force during the process of disarmament and demobilization.

3. UNOMSIL shall be present in all disarmament and demobilization locations to monitor the process and provide security guarantees to all ex-combatants.

4. Upon the signing of the present agreement, the government of Sierra Leone shall immediately request the international community to assist with the provision of the necessary financial and technical resources needed for the adaptation and extension of the existing Encampment, Disarmament, Demobilization, and Reintegration Program in Sierra Leone, including payment of retirement benefits and other emoluments due to former members of the SLA.

Article XVII: Restructuring and Training of the Sierra Leone Armed Forces

1. The restructuring, composition, and training of the new Sierra Leone armed forces will be carried out by the government with a view to creating truly national armed forces, bearing loyalty solely to the state of Sierra Leone, and able and willing to perform their constitutional role.

2. Those ex-combatants of the RUF/SL, CDF, and SLA who wish to be integrated into the new restructured national armed forces may do so provided they meet established criteria.

3. Recruitment into the armed forces shall reflect the geopolitical structure of Sierra Leone within the established strength.

Article XVIII: Withdrawal of Mercenaries

All mercenaries, in any guise, shall be withdrawn from Sierra Leone immediately upon the signing of the present agreement. Their withdrawal shall be supervised by the Joint Monitoring Commission.

Article XIX: Notification to Joint Monitoring Commission

Immediately upon the establishment of the JMC provided for in Article II of the present agreement, each party shall furnish to the JMC information regarding the strength and locations of all combatants as well as the positions and descriptions of all known unexploded bombs (UXBs), explosive ordnance devices (EODs), minefields, booby traps, wire entanglements, and all other physical or military hazards. The JMC shall seek all necessary technical assistance in mine clearance and the disposal or destruction of similar devices and weapons under the operational control of the neutral peacekeeping force. The parties shall keep the JMC updated on changes in this information so that it can notify the public as needed, to prevent injuries.

Article XX: Notification to Military Commands

Each party shall ensure that the terms of the present agreement, and written orders requiring compliance, are immediately communicated to all of its forces.

PART FIVE: HUMANITARIAN, HUMAN RIGHTS, AND SOCIOECONOMIC ISSUES

1. The Government of Sierra Leone and the RUF/SL, recognizing the importance of upholding, promoting and protecting the human rights of every Sierra Leonean as well as the enforcement of humanitarian law, agree to the following formulas for the achievement of these laudable objectives. Each of these formulas (not in priority order) is contained in separate Articles of this Part of the present Agreement.

Article XXI—Release of Prisoners and Abductees
Article XXII—Refugees and Displaced Persons
Article XXIII—Guarantee of the Security of Displaced Persons and Refugees
Article XXIV—Guarantee and Promotion of Human Rights
Article XXV—Human Rights Commission
Article XXVI—Human Rights Violations
Article XXVII—Humanitarian Relief
Article XXVIII—Postwar Rehabilitation and Reconstruction
Article XXIX—Special Fund for War Victims
Article XXX—Child Combatants
Article XXXI—Education and Health

Article XXI: Release of Prisoners and Abductees

All political prisoners of war as well as all non-combatants shall be released immediately and unconditionally by both parties, in accordance with the Statement of June 2, 1999, which is contained in Annex 3 and constitutes an integral part of the present agreement.

Article XXII: Refugees and Displaced Persons

The parties through the National Commission for Resettlement, Rehabilitation, and Reconstruction agree to seek funding from and the involvement of the UN and other agencies, including friendly countries, in order to design and implement a plan for voluntary repatriation and reintegration of Sierra Leonean refugees and internally displaced persons, including noncombatants, in conformity with international conventions, norms, and practices.

Article XXIII: Guarantee of the
Security of Displaced Persons and Refugees

As a reaffirmation of their commitment to the observation of the conventions and principles of human rights and the status of refugees, the parties shall take effective and appropriate measures to ensure that the right of Sierra Leoneans to asylum is fully respected and that no camps or dwellings of refugees or displaced persons are violated.

Article XXIV: Guarantee and Promotion of Human Rights

1. The basic civil and political liberties recognized by the Sierra Leone legal system and contained in the declarations and principles of human rights adopted by the UN and OAU, especially the Universal Declaration of Human Rights and the African Charter on Human and People's Rights, shall be fully protected and promoted within Sierra Leonean society.

2. These include the right to life and liberty, freedom from torture, the right to a fair trial, freedom of conscience, expression, and association, and the right to take part in the governance of one's country.

Article XXV: Human Rights Commission

1. The parties pledge to strengthen the existing machinery for addressing grievances of the people in respect of alleged violations of their basic human rights by the creation, as a matter of urgency and not later than ninety days after the signing of the present agreement, of an autonomous quasi-judicial national Human Rights Commission.

2. The parties further pledge to promote human rights education throughout the various sectors of Sierra Leonean society, including the schools, the media, the police, the military and the religious community.

3. In pursuance of the above, technical and material assistance may be sought from the UN High Commissioner for Human Rights, the African Commission on Human and Peoples Rights, and other relevant international organizations.

4. A consortium of local human rights and civil society groups in Sierra Leone shall be encouraged to help monitor human rights observance.

Article XXVI: Human Rights Violations

1. A Truth and Reconciliation Commission shall be established to address impunity, break the cycle of violence, provide a forum for both the victims and perpetrators of human rights violations to tell their story, and get a clear picture of the past in order to facilitate genuine healing and reconciliation.

2. In the spirit of national reconciliation, the commission shall deal with the question of human rights violations since the beginning of the Sierra Leonean conflict in 1991.

This commission shall, among other things, recommend measures to be taken for the rehabilitation of victims of human rights violations.

3. Membership of the commission shall be drawn from a cross-section of Sierra Leonean society with the participation and some technical support of the international community. This commission shall be established within ninety days after the signing of the present agreement and shall, not later than twelve months after the commencement of its work, submit its report to the government for immediate implementation of its recommendations.

Article XXVII: Humanitarian Relief

1. The parties reaffirm their commitment to their Statement on the Delivery of Humanitarian Assistance in Sierra Leone of June 3, 1999, which is contained in Annex 4 and constitutes an integral part of the present agreement. To this end, the government shall request appropriate international humanitarian assistance for the people of Sierra Leone who are in need all over the country.

2. The parties agree to guarantee safe and unhindered access by all humanitarian organizations throughout the country in order to facilitate delivery of humanitarian assistance, in accordance with international conventions, principles, and norms that govern humanitarian operations. In this respect, the parties agree to guarantee the security of the presence and movement of humanitarian personnel.

3. The parties also agree to guarantee the security of all properties and goods transported, stocked or distributed by humanitarian organizations, as well as the security of their projects and beneficiaries.

4. The government shall set up at various levels throughout the country, the appropriate and effective administrative or security bodies that will monitor and facilitate the implementation of these guarantees of safety for the personnel, goods, and areas of operation of the humanitarian organizations.

Article XXVIII: Postwar Rehabilitation and Reconstruction

1. The government, through the National Commission for Resettlement, Rehabilitation, and Reconstruction and with the support of the international community, shall provide appropriate financial and technical resources for postwar rehabilitation, reconstruction, and development.

2. Given that women have been particularly victimized during the war, special attention shall be accorded to their needs and potentials in formulating and implementing national rehabilitation, reconstruction, and development programs, to enable them to play a central role in the moral, social, and physical reconstruction of Sierra Leone.

Article XXIX: Special Fund for War Victims

The government, with the support of the international community, shall design and implement a program for the rehabilitation of war victims. For this purpose, a special fund shall be set up.

Article XXX: Child Combatants

The government shall accord particular attention to the issue of child soldiers. It shall, accordingly, mobilize resources, both within the country and from the international community, and especially through the office of the UN Special Representative for Children in Armed Conflict, UNICEF, and other agencies, to address the special needs of these children in the existing disarmament, demobilization, and reintegration processes.

Article XXXI: Education and Health

The government shall provide free compulsory education for the first nine years of schooling (Basic Education) and shall endeavor to provide free schooling for a further three years. The government shall also endeavor to provide affordable primary health care throughout the country.

PART SIX: IMPLEMENTATION OF THE AGREEMENT

Article XXXII: Joint Implementation Committee

A Joint Implementation Committee consisting of members of the Commission for the Consolidation of Peace (CCP) and the Committee of Seven on Sierra Leone, as well as the moral guarantors, provided for in

Article XXXIV of the present agreement, and other international supporters, shall be established. Under the chairmanship of ECOWAS, the Joint
Implementation Committee shall be responsible for reviewing and assessing the state of implementation of the agreement, and shall meet at least
once every three months. Without prejudice to the functions of the
Commission for the Consolidation of Peace as provided for in Article VI,
the Joint Implementation Committee shall make recommendations
deemed necessary to ensure effective implementation of the present
agreement according to the Schedule of Implementation, which appears
as Annex 5.

Article XXXIII: Request for International Involvement

The parties request that the provisions of the present agreement affecting
the United Nations shall enter into force upon the adoption by the UN
Security Council of a resolution responding affirmatively to the request
made in this agreement. Likewise, the decisionmaking bodies of the other
international organizations concerned are requested to take similar action,
where appropriate.

PART SEVEN: MORAL GUARANTORS
AND INTERNATIONAL SUPPORT

Article XXXIV: Moral Guarantors

The government of the Togolese Republic, the United Nations, the OAU,
ECOWAS, and the Commonwealth of Nations shall stand as moral guarantors that this peace agreement is implemented with integrity and in good
faith by both parties.

Article XXXV: International Support

Both parties call on the international community to assist them in implementing the present agreement with integrity and good faith. The international organizations mentioned in Article XXXIV and the governments of
Benin, Burkina Faso, Côte d'Ivoire, Ghana, Guinea, Liberia, Libyan Arab
Jamahiriya, Mali, Nigeria, Togo, the United Kingdom, and the United
States of America are facilitating and supporting the conclusion of this
agreement. These states and organizations believe that this agreement must
protect the paramount interests of the people of Sierra Leone in peace and
security.

PART EIGHT: FINAL PROVISIONS

Article XXXVI: Registration and Publication

The Sierra Leone government shall register the signed agreement not later than fifteen days from the date of the signing of this agreement. The signed agreement shall also be published in the *Sierra Leone Gazette* not later than forty-eight hours after the date of registration of this agreement. This agreement shall be laid before the parliament of Sierra Leone not later than twenty-one days after the signing of this agreement.

Article XXXVII: Entry into Force

The present agreement shall enter into force immediately upon its signing by the parties.

Done in Lomé this seven day of the month of July 1999 in twelve (12) original texts in English and French, each text being equally authentic.

Alhaji Ahmad Tejan Kabbah
President of the Republic of Sierra Leone
Corporal Foday Saybana Sankoh
Leader of the Revolutionary United Front of Sierra Leone
His Excellency Gnassingbe Eyadema
President of the Togolese Republic, Chairman of ECOWAS
His Excellency Blaise Compaore
President of Burkina Faso
His Excellency Dahkpanah Dr. Charles Ghankey Taylor
President of the Republic of Liberia
His Excellency Olusegun Obasanjo
President and Commander-in-Chief of the Armed Forces of the Federal Republic of Nigeria
His Excellency Youssoufou Bamba
Secretary of State at the Foreign Mission in Charge of International Cooperation of Côte d'Ivoire
His Excellency Victor Gbeho
Minister of Foreign Affairs of the Republic of Ghana
Mr. Roger Laloupo
Representative of the ECOWAS Special Representative
Ambassador Francis G. Okelo
Executive Secretary of the United Nations Secretary-General
Ms. Adwoa Coleman
Representative of the Organization of African Unity
Dr. Moses K. Z. Anafu
Representative of the Commonwealth of Nations

Annex 1: Agreement on Cease-Fire in Sierra Leone

President Ahmed Tejan Kabbah and Rev. Jesse Jackson met on May 18, 1999, with Corporal Foday Saybana Sankoh, under the auspices of President Gnassingbe Eyadema. At that meeting, the question of the peace process for Sierra Leone was discussed.

*   *   *

The government of the Republic of Sierra Leone and the Revolutionary United Front of Sierra Leone (RUF/SL),

Desirous to promote the ongoing dialogue process with a view to establishing durable peace and stability in Sierra Leone; and

Wishing to create an appropriate atmosphere conducive to the holding of peace talks in Lomæ, which began with the RUF internal consultations to be followed by dialogue between the government and the RUF;

Have jointly decided to:

1. Agree to cease-fire as from May 24, 1999, the day that President Eyadema invited foreign ministers of ECOWAS to discuss problems pertaining to Sierra Leone. It was further agreed that the dialogue between the government of Sierra Leone and RUF would commence on May 25, 1999;

2. Maintain their present and respective positions in Sierra Leone as of May 24, 1999; and refrain from any hostile or aggressive act that could undermine the peace process;

3. Commit to start negotiations in good faith, involving all relevant parties in the discussions, not later than May 25 in Lomæ;

4. Guarantee safe and unhindered access by humanitarian organizations to all people in need; establish safe corridors for the provision of food and medical supplies to ECOMOG soldiers behind RUF lines, and to RUF combatants behind ECOMOG lines;

5. Immediate release of all prisoners of war and noncombatants;

6. Request the United Nations, subject to the Security Council's authorization, to deploy military observers as soon as possible to observe compliance by the government forces (ECOMOG and Civil Defense Forces) and the RUF, including former AFRC forces, with this cease-fire agreement.

This agreement is without prejudice to any other agreement or additional protocols that may be discussed during the dialogue between the government and the RUF.

Signed in Lomæ (Togo) May 18, 1999, in six (6) originals in English and French.

For the government of Sierra Leone
    Alhadji Dr. Ahmad Tejan Kabbah
        President Of The Republic Of Sierra Leone

For the Revolutionary United Front Of Sierra Leone
    Corporal Foday Saybana Sankoh
        Leader of the Revolutionary United Front (RUF)
Witnessed By:
For the Government of Togo and Current Chairman of ECOWAS
    Gnassingbe Eyadema
        President of the Republic of Togo
For the United Nations
    Francis G. Okelo
        Special Representative of the Secretary General
For the Organization of African Unity (OAU)
    Adwoa Coleman
        Representative of the Organization of African Unity
U.S. Presidential Special Envoy for the Promotion of Democracy in Africa
    Rev. Jesse Jackson

Annex 2: Definition of Cease-Fire Violations

1. In accordance with Article II of the present agreement, both parties agree that the following constitute cease-fire violations and a breach of the Cease-Fire Agreement:

    a. The use of weapons of any kind in any circumstance including:

        (i) Automatic and semi-automatic rifles, pistols, machine guns and any other small arms weapon systems.

        (ii) Heavy machine guns and any other heavy weapon systems.

        (iii) Grenades and rocket-propelled grenade weapon systems.

        (iv) Artillery, rockets, mortars, and any other indirect fire weapon systems.

        (v) All types of mine, explosive devices, and improvised booby traps.

        (vi) Air defense weapon systems of any nature.

        (vii) Any other weapon not included in the above paragraphs.

    b. Troop movements of any nature outside of the areas recognized as being under the control of respective fighting forces without prior notification to the Cease-Fire Monitoring Committee of any movements at least forty-eight hours in advance.

    c. The movement of arms and ammunition. To be considered in the context of Security Council Resolution 1171 (1998).

    d. Troop movements of any nature.

    e. The construction and/or the improvement of defensive works and positions within respective areas of control, but outside a geographical boundary of 500 meters from existing similar positions.

 f. Reconnaissance of any nature outside of respective areas of control.

 g. Any other offensive or aggressive action.

2. Any training or other military activities not provided for in Articles XIII to XIX of the present agreement, constitute a cease-fire violation.

3. In the event of a hostile external force threatening the territorial integrity or sovereignty of Sierra Leone, military action may be undertaken by the Sierra Leone government.

Annex 3: Statement by the Government of Sierra Leone and the Revolutionary United Front of Sierra Leone on the Release of Prisoners of War and Noncombatants

The Government of Sierra Leone (GOSL) and the Revolutionary United Front (RUF/SL) have agreed to implement as soon as possible the provision of the Cease-Fire Agreement that was signed on May 18, 1999, in Lomæ, relating to the immediate release of prisoners of war and noncombatants.

Both sides reaffirmed the importance of the implementation of this provision in the interest of the furtherance of the talks.

They therefore decided that an appropriate committee is established to handle the release of all prisoners of war and noncombatants.

Both the Government of Sierra Leone and the Revolutionary United Front of Sierra Leone decided that such a committee be established by the UN and chaired by the UN Chief Military Observer in Sierra Leone and comprising representatives of the International Committee of the Red Cross (ICRC), UNICEF, and other relevant UN agencies and NGOs.

This committee should begin its work immediately by contacting both parties to the conflict with a view to effecting the immediate release of these prisoners of war and noncombatants.

—Lomé, June 2, 1999

Annex 4: Statement by the Government of Sierra Leone and the Revolutionary United Front of Sierra Leone on the Delivery of Humanitarian Assistance in Sierra Leone

The parties to the conflict in Sierra Leone meeting in Lomé, Togo, on June 3, 1999, in the context of the dialogue between the Government of Sierra Leone (GOSL) and the Revolutionary United Front of Sierra Leone (RUF/SL):

Reaffirm their respect for international convention, principles, and norms that govern the right of people to receive humanitarian assistance and the effective delivery of such assistance.

Reiterate their commitment to the implementation of the Cease-Fire Agreement signed by the two parties on May 18, 1999, in Lomæ.

Aware of the fact that the protracted civil strife in Sierra Leone has created a situation whereby the vast majority of Sierra Leoneans in need of humanitarian assistance cannot be reached.

Hereby agree as follows:

1. That all duly registered humanitarian agencies shall be guaranteed safe and unhindered access to all areas under the control of the respective parties in order that humanitarian assistance can be delivered safely and effectively, in accordance with international conventions, principles, and norms governing humanitarian operations.

2. In this respect the two parties shall:

   a. guarantee safe access and facilitate the fielding of independent assessment missions by duly registered humanitarian agencies.

   b. identify, in collaboration with the UN Humanitarian Coordinator in Sierra Leone and UNOMSIL, mutually agreed routes (road, air, and waterways) by which humanitarian goods and personnel shall be transported to the beneficiaries to provide needed assistance.

   c. allow duly registered humanitarian agencies to deliver assistance according to needs established through independent assessments.

   d. guarantee the security of all properties and of any goods transported, stocked, or distributed by the duly registered humanitarian agencies, as well as the security of their project areas and beneficiaries.

3. The two parties undertake to establish with immediate effect, and not later than seven days, an Implementation Committee formed by appropriately designated and mandated representatives from the Government of Sierra Leone, the Revolutionary United Front of Sierra Leone, the civil society, the NGO community, and UNOMSIL; and chaired by the United Nations Humanitarian Coordinator, in coordination with the special representative of the Secretary-General in Sierra Leone.

The Implementation Committee will be mandated to:

   a. Ascertain and assess the security of proposed routes to be used by the humanitarian agencies, and disseminate information on routes to interested humanitarian agencies.

   b. Receive and review complaints which may arise in the implementation of this arrangement, in order to reestablish full compliance.

4. The parties agree to set up at various levels in their areas of control, the appropriate and effective administrative and security bodies that will monitor and facilitate the effective delivery of humanitarian assistance in all approved points of delivery, and ensure the security of the personnel, goods, and project areas of the humanitarian agencies as well as the safety of the beneficiaries.

—Issued in Lomé, June 3, 1999

Selected Bibliography

Abdullah, Ibrahim. "Bush Path to Destruction: The Origins and Character of the Revolutionary United Front." *Journal of Modern African Studies* 36, no. 2 (1998).

Abdullah, Ibrahim, and Patrick K. Muana. "The Revolutionary United Front of Sierra Leone: A Revolt of the Lumpen Proletariat," in Christopher Clapham (ed.), *African Guerrillas*. Oxford: James Currey, 1998.

Abdullah, Ibrahim, and Yusuf Bangura (eds.). "Youth Culture and Political Violence: The Sierra Leone Civil War." *African Development* 22, nos. 2 and 3 (1997).

Abidjan Peace Accords. *Peace Agreement Between the Government of the Republic of Sierra Leone and the Revolutionary United Front of Sierra Leone.* Signed at Abidjan on November 30, 1996, S/1996/1034.

Address by his Excellency Alhaji Ahmad Tejan Kabbah, President of the Republic of Sierra Leone, to the 52nd Session of the UN General Assembly, Wednesday, October 1, 1997. Available online at www.sierra-leone.org/Kabbah100197.html.

Africa Confidential. "Chronology of Sierra Leone from 1991 to 1998: How Diamonds Fueled the Conflict." http://www.africa-confidential.com/sandline.html.

Africa Confidential 39, no. 21 (October 23, 1998): "Militias and Market Forces."

Africa Confidential 39, no. 18 (September 11, 1998): "Opening Up Aso Rock," 2.

African-American Institute. *Sierra Leone: A Final Report.* Washington, DC: The African-American Institute, December 1996.

Amnesty International. *Sierra Leone 1998—A Year of Atrocities Against Civilians.* AF 51/22/98. London: Amnesty International, November 1998.

Bangura, Yusuf. "Strategic Policy Failure and State Fragmentation: Security, Peacekeeping and Democratisation in Sierra Leone." Geneva: UN Research Institute for Social Development (UNRISD), 1999.

Cheney-Coker, Syl. "Agony of a State." Unpublished manuscript, September 1999.

Clapham, Christopher. "Recent History of Sierra Leone," in *Africa South of the Sahara 2000*. London: Europa, 1999.

Commonwealth. "Commonwealth Proposes Further Measures Against Military Regime in Nigeria," *Currents*, no. 2 (1996). Report of the Commonwealth Observer Group to the Presidential and Parliamentary Elections in Sierra Leone, April 1996.

Douglas, Ian. "Fighting for Diamonds: Private Military Companies in Sierra Leone," in Jakkie Cilliers and Peggy Mason (eds.), *Peace, Profit, or Plunder? The Privatisation of Security in War-Torn African Societies.* Johannesburg, South Africa: Institute for Security Studies, Halfway House, 1999.

Durch, William (ed.). *UN Peacekeeping: American Policy and the Uncivil Wars of the 1990s.* New York: St. Martin's Press, 1996.

ECOWAS. *ECOWAS Six-Month Peace Plan for Sierra Leone*, October 23, 1997, to April 22, 1998. Conakry: ECOWAS, October 23, 1997.

———. *Final Communiqué of the Summit of the Economic Community of West African States.* Held at Abuja on 28 and 29 August 1997. S/1997/695, September 8, 1997.

———. *First Report of the Economic Community of West African States Committee of Five on Sierra Leone to the Security Council Made Pursuant to Resolution 1132.* S/1997/895, November 17, 1997.

Gberie, Lansana. *War and State Collapse: The Case of Sierra Leone.* Waterloo, Ontario: Wilfred Laurier University Press, 1998.

Government of Sweden, Ministry of Foreign Affairs. *Preventing Violent Conflict: A Swedish Action Plan.* Stockholm: 1999.

Harbeson, John, and Donald Rothchild (eds.). *Africa in World Politics: The African State System in Flux*, 3d ed. Boulder, CO: Westview Press, 2000.

Hayward, Fred. "Sierra Leone: State Consolidation, Fragmentation, and Decay," in C. O'Brien, L. Cruise, R. Rathbone, and J. Dunn (eds.), *Contemporary West African States.* Cambridge: Cambridge University Press, 1989.

Hochschild, Adam. *King Leopold's Ghost: A Story of Greed, Terror and Heroism in Colonial Africa.* Boston: Houghton Mifflin, 1998.

Human Rights Watch. *Forgotten Children of War: Sierra Leonean Refugee Children in Guinea*, vol. 11, no. 5, July 1999.

———. *Sierra Leone: Sowing Terror—Atrocities Against Civilians in Sierra Leone*, vol. 10, no. 3, July 1998.

Kaplan, Robert. "The Coming Anarchy." *Atlantic Monthly*, February 1994.

Koroma, Abdul K. *Sierra Leone: The Agony of a Nation.* United Kingdom: Andromeda Publications, 1996.

Legg, Sir Thomas, KCB, QC, and Sir Robin Ibbs, KBE. "Report of the Sierra Leone Arms Investigation." London: The Stationery Office, July 27, 1998.

Lucan, Talabi A. *A Visual History of West Africa.* Ibadan, Nigeria: Evans Brothers Limited, 1981.

Médecins Sans Frontières. *Report: Overview of the Sierra Leone Crisis—the Humanitarian Situation Known to MSF*, July 1998. Brussels: MSF.

Mortimer, Robert. "From ECOMOG to ECOMOG II: Intervention in Sierra Leone," in John W. Harbeson and Donald Rothchild (eds.), *Africa in World Politics: The African State System in Flux*, 3d ed. Boulder, CO: Westview Press, 2000.

O'Brien, C., L. Cruise, R. Rathbone, and J. Dunn (eds.). *Contemporary West African States.* Cambridge: Cambridge University Press, 1989.

Opala, Joseph. "The People of Sierra Leone," *Sierra Leone: International Crisis Group Report to the Japanese Government.* Brussels: ICG, April 1996.

———."Sierra Leone: The Politics of State Collapse." Unpublished manuscript, Conference on Irregular Warfare in Liberia and Sierra Leone. SAIC, Denver, Colorado, July 30–August 1, 1998.

Reno, William. *Corruption and State Politics in Sierra Leone.* Cambridge: Cambridge University Press, 1995.

————.*Warlord Politics and African States.* Boulder, CO: Lynne Rienner Publishers, 1998.

Revolutionary United Front (RUF). "Footpath to Democracy," unpublished manuscript, 1995. Available online at www.sierra-leone.org.

————. "Lasting Peace in Sierra Leone: The Revolutionary United Front Sierra Leone (RUF/SL) Perspective and Vision," May 11, 1999. Available online at www.sierra-leone.org.

Richards, Paul. *Fighting for the Rain Forest: War, Youth, and Resources in Sierra Leone.* Oxford: James Currey, 1998.

————. "Rebellion in Liberia and Sierra Leone: A Crisis of Youth?" in O. W. Furley (ed.), *Conflict in Africa.* London: Tauris, 1995.

Riley, Steve. "Sierra Leone: The Militariat Strikes Again." *Review of African Political Economy,* no. 72 (1997).

Shawcross, William. *Deliver Us from Evil: Peacekeepers, Warlords, and a World of Endless Conflict.* New York: Simon and Schuster, 2000.

Shearer, David. "Private Armies and Military Intervention." *IISS Adelphi Paper 316.* Oxford: Oxford University Press, 1998.

Smillie, Ian, Lansana Gberie, and Ralph Hazelton. *The Heart of the Matter: Sierra Leone, Diamonds, and Human Security.* Toronto: Partnership Africa/Canada, 2000.

Sørbø, Gunner, Joanna Macrae, and Lennart Wohlgemuth. "NGOs in Conflict: An Evaluation of International Alert," Chr. Michelsen Institute Report Series, No. 6. Bergen, Norway: CMI, 1997.

Strategic Studies. *The Military Balance 1997/98.* Oxford: Oxford University Press, 1997.

United Nations Development Programme. Human Development Index (HDI) in *Human Development Report 1999: Globalization with a Human Face.* New York: United Nations, July 12, 1999.

United Nations High Commissioner for Refugees (UNHCR). "Refugee Population by Country of Asylum and Origin, 1997–1998," *Refugees and Others of Concern to UNHCR—1998 Statistical Overview,* 1998. Geneva: UNHCR.

United Nations Humanitarian Assistance Coordination Unit for Sierra Leone. "Sierra Leone Humanitarian Situation Report," Special Issue, March 7, 2000.

United Nations, Office for the Coordination of Humanitarian Affairs. "Sierra Leone: IRIN Special Report on Demobilization," July 9, 1999. Available online at www.reliefweb.int/IRIN.

United Nations Secretariat. *Address to the Annual Assembly of Heads of State and Government of the Organization of African Unity.* Harare, SG/SM6245 AFR/9, June 2, 1997.

United Nations Security Council. *The Fourth Report of the Secretary-General on the United Nations Mission in Sierra Leone.* S/2000/455, May 19, 2000.

————. *Letter from the Secretary-General Addressed to the President of the Security Council.* S/1997/776, October 7, 1997.

————. *Report of the Secretary-General on Sierra Leone.* S/1997/80, January 26, 1997.

————. Statement by the President of the Security Council, July 11, 1997, S/PRST/1997/36.

————. Resolution 1270. S/RES/1270, October 22, 1999.

————. Resolution 1289. S/RES/1289, February 7, 2000.

———. Resolution 1132. S/RES/1132, October 8, 1997.

———. *Second Report of the Secretary-General on the Situation in Sierra Leone.* S/1997/958, December 5, 1997.

———. Secretary-General's Report to the UN Security Council, "The Causes of Conflict and the Promotion of Durable Peace and Sustainable Development in Africa," April 16, 1998.

———. *Seventh Report of the Secretary-General on the United Nations Observer Mission in Sierra Leone.* S/1999/836, July 30, 1999.

———. *Third Report of the Secretary-General on the Situation in Sierra Leone.* S/1998/103, February 5, 1998.

———. *Second Report of the Secretary-General Pursuant to Security Council Resolution 1270 (1999) on the United Nations Mission in Sierra Leone.* S/2000/13, January 11, 2000.

———. *Third Report of the Secretary-General on the United Nations Mission in Sierra Leone.* S/2000/186, March 7, 2000.

———. *Fourth Report of the Secretary-General on the United Nations Mission in Sierra Leone.* S/2000/455, May 19, 2000.

U.S. Congress. H. Con. Res. 99. 105th U.S. Congress, June 16, 1997.

U.S. Congress. H.R. 3879, Sierra Leone Peace Support Act of 2000. Introduced in the House of Representatives, March 9, 2000.

Van der Laan, H. L. *The Lebanese Traders of Sierra Leone.* The Hague/Paris: Mouton, 1975.

Zack-Williams, Alfred B. *Tributors, Supporters and Merchant Capital: Mining and Underdevelopment in Sierra Leone.* London: Avebury, 1995.

———. "Kamajors, 'Sobel' and the Militariat: Civil Society and the Return of the Military in Sierra Leone Politics." *Review of African Political Economy* 24 (1997).

Zack-Williams, A. B., and Steve Riley. "Sierra Leone: The Coup and Its Consequences." *Review of African Political Economy*, no. 56 (1993).

Zartman, William I. (ed.). *Collapsed States: The Disintegration and Restoration of Legitimate Authority.* Boulder, CO: Lynne Rienner Publishers, 1995.

Index

on Sierra Leone, 64–65; support
from, 99–100
United Nations Observer Mission in
Sierra Leone (UNOMSIL), 83, 86,
87, 89, 96, 101, 102, 103, 104, 109,
110, 124, 127, 128, 130
United States, 85; aid to Liberia, 32;
assistance to Sierra Leone, 97; criticism of, 88; diplomatic efforts, 79;
economic assistance from, 109; emi-
gration to, 30; engagement in Africa,
63; in peace operations, 59–61; policy on Sierra Leone, 102; special
envoys, 81; Special Forces, 68$n16$,
109; withdrawal from Africa, 17
UNOMSIL. *See* United Nations
Observer Mission in Sierra Leone

USS Kearsarge, 59, 120
U.S. State Department, 13, 58, 74

War criminals, 104
Warlords, 96
"West Side Boys," 133
Wimhurst, David, 130
Wolf, Frank R., 102, 107$n8$
Women's movement, 40
World Bank, 44, 100, 101, 123
World Diamond Congress, 133
World Food Program, 57
World Vision, 66
Wright, Ann, 58, 59

Zaire, 59
Zambia, 127

About the Publication

Sierra Leone's bitter experience with civil war garnered international attention only after the May 1997 coup, though the conflict between the Revolutionary United Front (RUF) and successive governments has raged for at least a decade—against the backdrop of more than three decades of progressive state collapse. John Hirsch traces Sierra Leone's downward spiral, drawing on his firsthand experience as U.S. ambassador in Freetown in 1995–1998.

Hirsch analyzes the historical, social, and economic contexts of the ongoing struggle, as well as the impact of regional and international powers. Topics covered include the exploitation of mineral resources in the country, the involvement of private security forces, and the flawed efforts at peace negotiations. Without sustained international intervention, he cautions, it is unlikely that Sierra Leone—a microcosm of much of Africa's post–Cold War experience—can achieve stability and a renewal of democratic institutions.

John L. Hirsch joined the International Peace Academy as vice president after serving for more than thirty years with the U.S. Foreign Service, most recently in Sierra Leone. He is also director of the International Fellows Program at Columbia University's School of International and Public Affairs. Dr. Hirsch is coauthor of *Somalia and Operation Restore Hope: Reflections on Peacemaking and Peacekeeping*.

Other International Peace Academy Publications

Available from Lynne Rienner Publishers, 1800 30th Street, Boulder, Colorado 80301 (303-444-6684):

The Wave of the Future: The United Nations and Naval Peacekeeping, Robert Stephens Staley II (1992)

Political Order in Post-Communist Afghanistan, William Maley and Fazel Haq Saikal (1992)

UN Peacekeeping in Cambodia, Michael W. Doyle (1995)

Rights and Reconciliation: UN Strategies in El Salvador, Ian Johnstone (1995)

Building Peace in Haiti, Chetan Kumar (1998)

Greed and Grievance: Economic Agendas in Civil War, edited by Mats Berdal and David Malone (2000)

The Sanctions Decade: Assessing UN Strategies in the 1990s, David Cortright and George A. Lopez (2000)

Peacebuilding as Politics: Cultivating Peace in Fragile Societies, edited by Elizabeth M. Cousens and Chetan Kumar (2001)

The International Peace Academy

The International Peace Academy (IPA) is an independent, nonpartisan, international institution devoted to the promotion of peaceful and multilateral approaches to the resolution of international as well as internal conflicts. IPA plays a facilitating role in efforts to settle conflicts, providing a middle ground where the options for settling particular conflicts are explored and promoted in an informal setting. Other activities of the organization include public forums; training seminars on conflict resolution and peacekeeping; and research and workshops on collective security, regional and internal conflicts, peacemaking, peacekeeping, and nonmilitary aspects of security.

In fulfilling its mission, IPA works closely with the United Nations, regional and other organizations, governments, and parties to conflicts. The work of IPA is further enhanced by its ability to draw on a worldwide network of eminent persons including government leaders, statesmen, business leaders, diplomats, military officers, and scholars. In the decade following the end of the Cold War, there has been a general awakening to the enormous potential of peaceful and multilateral approaches to resolving conflicts. This has given renewed impetus to the role of IPA.

IPA is governed by an international board of directors. Financial support for the work of the organization is provided primarily by philanthropic foundations, as well as individual donors.